Finding Time

COLLECTION ON

TECHNOLOGY and **WORK**

edited by **STEPHEN R. BARLEY**

Finding Time

How Corporations, Individuals, and Families Can Benefit from New Work Practices

Leslie A. Perlow

ILR Press, an imprint of
Cornell University Press

ITHACA AND LONDON

First published 1997 by Cornell University Press.
First printing, Cornell Paperbacks, 1997.

Printed in the United States of America

Library of Congress Cataloging-in-Publication Data

Perlow, Leslie A., 1967–
    Finding Time : how corporations, individuals, and families can
benefit from new work practices / Leslie A. Perlow
        p.   cm.
    Includes bibliographical references and index.
    ISBN 0-8014-3425-4 (cloth : alk. paper). — ISBN 0-8014-8445-6
(pbk. : alk. paper)
        1. Hours of labor. 2. Work and family. 3. Quality of life.
    4. Leisure.   I. Title.
    ND5106.P42   1997
    331.25'7—DC21   97-14969

Cornell University Press strives to utilize environmentally responsible suppliers and materials to the fullest extent possible in the publishing of its books. Such materials include vegetable-based, low-VOC inks and acid-free papers that are also either recycled, totally chlorine-free, or partly composed of nonwood fibers.

Cloth printing 10 9 8 7 6 5 4 3 2 1

Paperback printing 10 9 8 7 6 5 4 3 2 1

In loving memory of
Uncle Bob
who taught me
the preciousness of time

Contents

Foreword

My father, who quit high school in his junior year during the Great Depression to thresh wheat for a free meal and a quarter a day, understood what it meant to work long past the point when his muscles were sore. By the time I was born, he had also learned what it was like to punch a time clock and work a second job to make ends meet. Dad thought that if the school of hard knocks had taught him anything, it was the value of an education, and he was deeply committed to making sure my sister and I took school more seriously than he had. I was six when he first shared his vision of why he wanted me to be educated and, by implication, white collar. We were in the garage where Dad had his workbench and what must have been every hand tool known to man. On this particular day, he had torn down the I-6 of his '53 BelAire hoping to save money by grinding his own valves. I don't remember Dad's precise words, but I know he made four points because he made those same four points over and over for ten years until it became clear that I would not only graduate from high school but go to college as well. An education was critical, went Dad's mantra, because it meant a "clean job," "good money," "not having to take orders from fools," and having the time to "do what you want, because you won't have to work as hard as I do." He'd summarize succinctly, "With a college education you'll have it made in the shade."

Although Dad eventually took great pride in telling his buddies that I worked for universities that Dan Rather mentioned on the evening news, he never really understood why I kept going back to school after I received a bachelor's degree. He had assumed college was a four-year proposition. But what he found even more incomprehensible was why so much schooling hadn't paid off, at least by any reckoning he understood. One day, a few years before he died, I found myself telling him that I didn't think I'd be able to visit because I had so much work to do. He said, "Don't worry, you don't always get to do what you want. A man's gotta work. Besides, you've got a family and they come first. But, you know, I thought if you went to college you wouldn't have to work so hard. Seems like you're always working. Sometimes I think you work harder than I did. What happened?" "Good question," I squirmed uncomfortably; "wish I knew."

I suspect a large portion of the generation born in the fifties and schooled in the sixties frequently ask themselves Dad's question. Many of us were told that with a college education, appropriate technology, and a heightened awareness of what matters, we could have a challenging career, a fulfilling family life, and sufficient time left over to enjoy a little recreation and even contribute to the greater good. Some people, like my father, thought more leisure would come naturally as machines took away drudgery and the standard of living rose. With a refrigerator in every kitchen, a TV in every living room, a vacuum cleaner in every closet, a car in every garage, a college degree, and a world made safe for democracy, who could help but find the time to enjoy a well-rounded life? Those of us who were more skeptical of blind progress and the good will of our leaders naively thought that once we were in charge, we'd create the sense of balance that the system so sorely lacked. Among other things, we'd banish organization men once and for all and replace their grey flannel suits with pairs of jeans.

Wandering the cubicles of high tech firms in the Silicon Valley where engineers and computer scientists commune with CRTs, one sees plenty of jeans. But stare beyond the Levis and you'll see that lives in the Silicon Valley (like lives in Boston, Columbus, or almost anywhere else) look uncannily like the lives that so many of us swore not to recapitulate. The primary differences seem to be that organization women have now joined the ranks of organization men, that the two are often married to each other, at least for a while, and that as a result, almost nobody has sufficient time for anybody else, including the children.

If you listen closely in the cafes and bars in towns like Palo Alto, Sunnyvale, and Cupertino, you'll hear people longing for a time clock to punch. You'll hear people complain about never having "quality" time with their spouse or children. You might even conclude that finding adequate child care is a collective obsession.

In fact, these white-collar people in jeans and tee shirts, whom we call knowledge workers, sometimes seem to be so busy that you begin to wonder when they found time to procreate in the first place.

What happened may be that we never grasped what our parents thought they had lost: the freedom to do what you want with your time. If our parents were neither professionals nor managers, they may even have had more time than we do. This was what my Dad concluded: he had had more time than I did. If you're "nonexempt"—if you punch a time clock or fill out a time card—you may not be able to make ends meet or even decide how you will work. You may become bored and purely instrumental about your job. But you can usually count on when the day will start and when it will end. You can also usually count on having most of your evenings and weekends to yourself. So if you don't work a second job, then you generally have no one but yourself to blame if you don't have time for your family or yourself. Such are the benefits of knowing precisely what you owe your employer and what your employer owes you. In the world of nonexempts, employers and employees alike know they have forty hours to conclude a week's exchange unless, of course, the former want to pay overtime.

Those who study labor relations say that controlling time is key to the struggle over who controls the labor process. It was for this reason that one of the labor movement's primary objectives in the first half of the twentieth century was to restrict how much time employers could legally demand of their employees. The fight for the forty-hour week limited exploitation by drawing a sharp boundary between work and nonwork, a boundary that didn't exist prior to the industrial revolution. But the boundary was never drawn sharply for exempt employees. Managers, engineers, and other salaried professionals have always experienced fuzzier temporal boundaries than have blue-collar and lower white-collar workers. But because students of work previously focused most of their attention on the blue-collar labor force (or relatively independent professionals such as doctors and lawyers), they have only recently begun to see the troubles with which managers and engineers have long struggled privately. The decline of unionized labor, downsizing, the rise of contingent labor, the shift to a managerial, professional, and technical work force, the spread of high-commitment work cultures, and perhaps most important, the mass entry of women into the labor force have reheated issues of temporal control by blurring the boundary between the work and nonwork lives of a growing number of people. The most visible development is the epidemic of "work and family issues" that plague the lives of most people who drive BMWs and a large percentage of those who don't.

Social commentary on the demands of work falls roughly into two camps. The human-resource and self-help camp implicitly assumes that individuals are ultimately responsible for their own boundaries. The solution to work and family problems, therefore, lies in helping people learn to cope more effectively. The burgeoning market for advice on how to manage stress and time testifies not only to the scope of the problem but to the popularity of defining the problem as an individual issue. A smaller and more critical literature argues that time pressures are symptomatic not of people's failure to cope but of the increased sophistication of organizations in extracting surplus value. Rather than rely on coercion or bureaucracy, modern firms have learned to induce effort by manipulating values, cognitions, aspirations, and expectations. Under this new regime of "normative" or "concertive" control, as it is sometimes called, employees discipline themselves, thereby enabling organizations to afford compassion.

The problem is that real people resemble neither the dopes nor the dupes who populate these perspectives. The self-help literature would have us believe that our problems occur because we are inadequate, uninformed, or undisciplined, and the critical literature tells us we are pawns. Moreover, in the final analysis, both schools of thought are impractical: they offer simplistic solutions or no solution at all. The self-help and human-resource literature would have us believe that we can fix work family problems by demanding flextime and reorganizing ourselves. The critical literature all too often implies that the problem can't be fixed because the powerful are too powerful or the system too hegemonic. Leslie Perlow's analysis of how engineers in a bustling high tech firm use their time helps us see why neither account satisfies.

Perlow creates a complex and striking portrait of temporal purgatory by giving people voice. Amid the pages of *Finding Time* you will encounter engineers, spouses, and managers struggling to balance the demands of work and family. Like most good ethnographers, Perlow not only tells us what people say, she shows us what they do. As a result we get to see how people sometimes forge the chains by which others bind them. The people you are about to encounter author their realities, sometimes wittingly and sometimes unwittingly, but always in an interpersonal dance loaded with conflict, uncertainty, and a dash of unanticipated consequences. Nor is Perlow's organization as guiltless or as guilty as the human-resource and critical literatures respectively suggest. Instead, in *Finding Time* we encounter a complex sociocultural system that is neither immune nor readily amenable to change. By serving up slices of everyday life, Perlow shows us why it is so hard, but not impossible, to do something about overwork.

Although Perlow writes about engineers, their spouses, and their managers, in her stories most readers will see reflections of themselves. *Finding Time* transcends its specific subject, the troubles of a technical labor force, to become a kind of parable for our times with many lessons to teach. Let me whet your appetite for the text, by calling attention to several.

With my labor relations background I am perhaps too ready to believe that managers have a visible hand in creating the time pressures that people experience at work. Perlow's data leavens such a perspective. Sometimes her managers do make heartless demands, fully cognizant that their expectations for working nights and weekends will strain the engineers' relations with their families. They also actively sideline the careers of engineers who refuse to play temporal games by their rules. But most of the time, managers seem to muddle along, causing temporal trouble without knowing it. Over the course of the book we encounter managers who constantly interrupt engineers and call meetings at ungodly hours because they believe they need to be "statused" on how the work is progressing. The engineers have to quit what they're doing to "status" their managers because their managers have been told to "status" their managers and so on, presumably all the way up the stack of turtles to Yertle. We also encounter managers who stand over engineers as they work, especially when deadlines are tight and folks are pulling late-nighters. But most of these managers seem to be peering over the engineers' shoulders not because they want to monitor their minions, but because they believe either that they can help or that leadership requires making the same sacrifice they ask of their engineers. The irony, then, is that even with good intentions, management practices may succeed in exacerbating what everyone seeks to avoid: work that takes too long and never gets done on time. The simple fact is that when engineers are meeting management's need for communication, they can't attend to the technical tasks they are supposed to complete. Thus, in sharp contrast to what the gurus of innovation preach, one comes away from Perlow's account wondering if there isn't too much communication going on in research and development labs.

Yet managers aren't the only people who disrupt work in the name of communication. Engineers do too. Perlow's informants tell us over and over that they are constantly interrupting and being interrupted by other engineers in a seemingly never-ending search for help. Those who give help are rarely rewarded. Those who refuse to give help, but nevertheless seek it, often are. Yet helping turns out to be critical for the team as a whole because, like managers, few engineers have sufficient knowledge to do their jobs by themselves and because the work of all the engineers must come together in the product, the ultimate goal of the work. Thus, engineers join managers in creating an interactional milieu in which work is constantly being disrupted by almost everyone, exacerbating temporal pressures and, in turn, increasing the need to be statused and to seek help without helping.

Unlike most treatises on temporal strains and work/family problems, Perlow's book not only implies that the situation could be different, it demonstrates a simple technique for making it so. Perlow took a step exceedingly rare for a participant observer: she persuaded her informants to conduct an experiment. For more than a month, her informants and their managers set aside three mornings of quiet time each week. During these periods, interruptions were banned and engineers were allowed to work continuously on technical matters. When the experiment was over, not only were engineers and managers more satisfied but more work had been accomplished on time. Everyone, including the organization itself, appeared to benefit when engineers and managers interrupted each other less. Yet, in the end, the engineers did not reallocate the time they found to their families, and the team was unable to sustain the intervention on its own. Why? The uncomfortable answer is that the insidious temporal sink was sustained by taken-for-granted understandings of effort, work, and careers which made it difficult for managers and engineers to free themselves, even when a path to freedom was demonstrated. I won't spoil your read by telling you how the culture works—this is something for you to puzzle through with Perlow—but I will suggest that after reading Perlow's accounts, I suspect Pogo knew the answer to my Dad's question all along: "I's seen the enemy and they is us." If temporal problems are cultural problems, they are by nature systemic, but it is only through our own behaviors that the system survives.

STEPHEN R. BARLEY
Stanford, California

Preface

Anyone striving for success in today's professional world knows that long hours are a requirement of the job. This fact is well accepted. So are its consequences. Many men and women, married and single, with "too much to do and not enough time to do it" must make sacrifices in their lives outside of work. Work/family conflict has become a prominent social issue in the United States. In the last few years, almost every major newspaper and magazine has run a cover story on the consequences of overwork in America.[1] Among the most frequently mentioned are stress, exhaustion, divorce, and child neglect.

Despite these negative effects, people do not question the corporation's need for its employees to work long hours. Individuals may decide that the tradeoffs are not worth it, but they do not question whether long hours are in the corporation's best interest. In a recent book, *The Time Bind*, Arlie Russell Hochschild suggests that some people actually want to work these long hours. She argues that the work place has been transformed by new management techniques into a supportive, appreciative place that offers a welcome refuge from the tantrums, quarrels, and household chores that pervade domestic life. Ironically, however, these pressures, stresses, and irritants of home life are only exacerbated by the exorbitant amount of time people spend at work.

The question left unresolved by Hochschild and the many others who have documented the prevalence of long work hours and explored both their causes and consequences is what underlies the "time bind" itself. It is taken for granted that in the global marketplace, where speed is critical to a corporation's success, employees must put extensive amounts of time into their work. A simple assumption guides behavior: the longer employees work the better

---

[1] For recent articles in the popular press on overwork in America, see, for example, "Welcome to the Age of Overwork," *Fortune*, November 30, 1992; "Got a Minute," *New York Times*, April 24, 1994; "Breaking Point," *Newsweek*, March 6, 1995; "Time Out," *US News and World Report*, December 11, 1995; "Too Many Things to Do, Too Little Time to Do Them," *Wall Street Journal*, March 8, 1996; and "Good for the Bottom Line," *Time*, May 20, 1996.

the corporation will do. I set out to explore whether this assumption that organizational success is inextricably linked to long work hours is valid. Do people really need to work so hard or might organizations achieve even higher levels of marketplace success in other, less destructive ways? If the latter case turns out to be possible, then individuals, families, and organizations might all benefit from rethinking the way time is used at work.

My findings are based on the experiences of a group of software engineers, but a wide range of professionals including lawyers, consultants, investment bankers, and managers will likely find parallels to their own situations and benefit from the exploration of possible alternatives. This book tells a sad and, I am afraid, all too common tale, of a work force that suffers the consequences of long work hours, under the assumption that accommodation to work demands will bring both personal and corporate success. I have found, on the contrary, that those who work the hardest do not necessarily contribute most to the corporation's productivity and, in fact, that often no one benefits from this behavior, not even the corpora-tion. Managers, professionals, employees, family members, change consultants, advocates of work/family initiatives, and academics have reason to be optimistic. Change that improves both the corporation's bottom line and balance in individuals' lives is indeed possible.

My interest in this research stems from my own personal experiences. After graduating from college, I worked for a management consulting firm. The hours were terrible, but even worse, I had no control over my life. I might have accepted that I was going to have only one free night each week, had I only been able to predict which night it would be. I finally gave up trying to make plans with friends outside of work; it simply wasn't worth always having to cancel them.

This period of my life led to an important insight. I found that my peers and managers were working long hours because they believed that these hours were essential for the consulting firm, if not for their own success. I, however, suspected that if we had the incentive to get the work done in less time, we could create alternative ways of working that would be more efficient and effective. I was too junior to make a difference in that firm, and eventually I left, but I never forgot what I had come to realize about long work hours.

In 1991, Lotte Bailyn offered me an opportunity to join her on a new research project funded by the Ford Foundation to explore what it is about work that perpetuates work/life conflicts. It was my chance to examine systematically whether my insight from years before was indeed applicable to a Fortune 500 corporation. I was able to explore whether new work practices could be created which would benefit corporations, individuals, and families and what such change might entail.

This book has been a long time in the making and involved the unwavering support of many people along the way. To all of them, I am deeply grateful.

First, a special thanks is due to Lotte Bailyn for her leadership, advice, and support throughout this project. Thanks are also due to all the members of our research team including Deborah Kolb, Susan Eaton, Joyce Fletcher, Maureen Harvey, and Robin Johnson as well as our consultant, Rhona Rapoport. Thanks also to June Zeitlin, who oversaw the funding from the Ford Foundation and the Society of Scholars at the University of Michigan which provided further funding while I revised the manuscript.

Without the cooperation of the software engineers I studied this project would never have been possible. They welcomed me into their workplace and their homes and shared much of their precious time with me. I could not have asked for more friendly, receptive people to study.

Thanks are also due to Gideon Kunda for the multiple ways that he facilitated the writing of this book, from first introducing me to my editor to providing a thorough set of comments on the final manuscript. Wayne Baker, Jane Dutton, Mauro Guillen, Robert Quinn, and Karl Weick have all given much needed guidance throughout this process. My editor at Cornell University Press, Frances Benson, helped greatly in creating the final product.

My friends and family from all realms of the work world have provided invaluable feedback. Andrea Campbell, Nancy Katz,

Stephanie Mackie Lewis, Sarah Turner, and Denise Zarrin each read the complete manuscript. Heather Mcphee offered endless editorial and structural suggestions.

My teachers at the Massachusetts Institute of Technology (and Harvard University)—Lotte Bailyn, John Van Maanen, Nitin Nohria, and Deborah Kolb—created an educational experience for which I will always be grateful. Without them, I would still be struggling to figure out how to conduct fieldwork, how to make sense of thousands of pages of field notes, and how to craft a coherent tale.

Ron Fortgang provided not only insightful comments but much needed encouragement and understanding through the trials and tribulations as the book neared completion and we were thousands of miles away in countries where time took on a very different meaning. He helped me adjust as we learned that concepts such as "hurry" and "rigid deadline" simply did not exist.

Joy Perlow has supported this endeavor in countless ways from making valuable suggestions to providing endless love and support.

The contributions of John Van Maanen and Jon Perlow deserve to be singled out. They both read more versions of this book than I would like to admit existed and commented endlessly on everything from big ideas to small grammatical issues. Without them, the book simply would not be the same. Many many thanks.

LESLIE A. PERLOW
Ann Arbor, Michigan

INTRODUCTION

The Case against Long Work Hours

Max arrives at work early in the morning and stays until ten or eleven at night.[1] He often works eighty or ninety hours a week. When there is a crisis, Max drops everything in his personal life. He says, "My work is crucial, and I am willing to put in whatever hours the work demands."

In contrast to Max, who is single and has few demands on his time outside of work, Laura is married and has three young children. She too puts in exceedingly long hours at work, but she is tormented by the tradeoffs that are constantly required. Laura describes her priorities as "wishy washy. I want both a successful career and quantity time [*sic*] with my children. . . . I feel like I need more time, more time at home and more time at work. . . . Family is my first priority. . . . I wake up often in the middle of the night and think to myself, it does not matter if you're a superstar. I want to be less stressed. . . . But I am too internally competitive for that. I cannot stand not being at the top."

Many of us display the characteristics of Max and Laura. We work hard because we want to succeed. We may question whether this way of working makes sense for ourselves and our

---

[1] To protect the identity of the company and its employees, all names used are pseudonyms. All facts, however, throughout the book are accurate to the best of my knowledge.

families, but we do not ask whether the criteria of success are in the best interest of our work teams, our organizations, and our society. The assumption is that our styles of working, however destructive of family life, further the goals of our organizations. Max and Laura certainly believe that. They work hard because they want to succeed, but also because they want the product they are developing and ultimately the corporation for which they work to succeed.

My book explores this taken-for-granted assumption. I examine whether a system that rewards long hours and substantial sacrifices in life outside of work indeed serves to maximize the corporation's efficiency and profitability. Might there be alternative ways of working which would enable people to spend less time at work and yet improve the corporation's bottom line?

Long Work Hours

One need only read Tracy Kidder's *Soul of a New Machine*, which describes the creation of a thirty-two-bit minicomputer to grasp the intensity with which people work and the respect granted those who make this kind of commitment. As Diane Fassel notes in her book *Working Ourselves to Death*, we have "a social structure that rewards work addiction" (p. 4). Corporate lawyers, investment bankers, computer programmers, engineers, and many other professionals are expected to work seventy- or eighty-hour weeks routinely, and even longer during particularly hectic times. The grueling schedules once characteristic only of senior executives have become common in one occupation after another.[2]

This rise in the number of individuals expected to work long hours has been driven by a demand for increasingly complex, analytic, abstract work. The division of labor in the United States is shifting away from blue-collar work toward technical and professional work. The number of professional and technical jobs has in-

---

[2] William Whyte (1956) documented a large discrepancy between the work hours of organization men and senior executives. In Perlow forthcoming I describe the change over the past fifty years.

creased 300 percent since 1950. A quarter of all new jobs currently being created in the United States are either professional or technical in nature (Silvestri and Lukasiewicz 1991).

Daniel Bell (1973) suggests that the "workers" who fill these jobs cannot be managed like blue-collar workers; compulsion will not generate the necessary commitment, responsibility, and knowledge. Some, like Edward Lawler (1986), maintain that a new form of "high involvement management" is required to encourage individuals to contribute to and reap greater satisfaction from their work. Managers as a result feel pressure to promote both trust and openness at work.

At the same time that managers are granting these workers—often referred to as knowledge workers because of the heavy cognitive component of their jobs—more freedom and responsibility at work, however, they are increasing demands on their time. To receive raises and promotions, knowledge workers must demonstrate unlimited devotion to and energy for work. Knowledge workers, like senior executives, experience immense pressure to be at work and to put work above all else.

The work demands have increased concurrently with a significant change in the demographics of the work force. More employees than ever have responsibilities outside of work. Consider the following statistics. In 1960, 61 percent of married couples consisted of a working husband and a wife who was a full-time homemaker; by 1990 only 25 percent of married couples fit this description. During the same period, the percentage of dual-career couples with both spouses working full-time increased from 28 percent to 54 percent (Hayghe and Cromartie 1991).

Not only are more women entering the labor market, but a growing number of women are rising into professional and managerial ranks.[3] These women are subject to the same work ethic that demands long and unpredictable hours of men, but most women who work also have primary responsibility for child care

[3] From 1972 to 1990, the percentage of women working in executive, administrative, and managerial occupations increased from 20 percent to 40 percent; the proportion of women in professional specialty occupations rose from 44 percent to 51 percent. In particular, the percentage of female physicians rose from 10 percent to 19 percent, lawyers from 4 percent to 21 percent, and computer programmers from 20 percent to 26 percent (Hayghe and Cromartie, 1991).

and household chores. The combined demands of work and home on women, particularly those in dual-career relationships, have become exceedingly high. For men who share the responsibilities at home the burden is also great. Even those men who do not equally share home responsibilities experience marital stress and demands to help at home (Hochschild 1989). Recently, researchers have documented the simultaneous increase in demands on employees' time both at work and at home. Juliet Schor in *The Overworked American,* totals the hours of work both inside and outside the home, and, she concludes individuals are working an extra month a year.

The Price of Success

The consequences of the demand for long hours are severe. Paul Evans and Fernando Bartolome in their book *Must Success Cost So Much?* document the "life investments"—the time and energy, the emotional spillover, and the effects on marriage and family life—involved in the pursuit of success. They warn individuals about the costs of "being blinded by ambition" and emphasize the synergy of private and professional life. They further encourage organizations to alter their policies and practices to help employees better balance their professional and private lives. They suggest to managers that employees with balanced lives are more productive.

Similarly, in *Working Ourselves to Death,* Diane Fassel labels workaholism, the addiction to work, "a killer disease" and describes the types of workaholics, their characteristics, the progression of the disease, and its effects on families and the organization. She concludes that "it is an illusion to believe that work addicts benefit companies." Instead, she insists, organizations spend money rectifying workaholics' mistakes; they pay increased health care bills for stressed out employees; they see creativity and productivity drop as late-stage workaholics become forgetful and capable only of one-dimensional thinking; and they have more difficulty attracting gifted workers because consciously healthy people avoid settings that promote overwork (p. 141). Indeed, Fassel writes: "every week my office receives letters from people in organizations who are recovering from work addiction. The letters carry one of two themes: I got healthy, my family is getting healthy, but my workplace is workaholic. I go to work and I feel crazy. I am considering leaving. The other theme goes: I got healthy and I got fired. Conclusion: workaholic organizations are losing or getting rid of some of their healthiest people" (p. 145).

The corporate world has largely ignored this body of research and its conclusion that overwork has long-term costs for the organization, not just for individuals and their families. The lack of attention is not surprising. Increasing hours of work may be causing individual, family, societal, and even organizational problems, but managers consider long hours necessary to achieve organizational objectives. In a world where getting to market first has become a major determinant of organizational success, speed is seen as critical (Stalk and Hout 1990; Tucker 1991). Long hours are therefore viewed as a consequence of global competition.

Organizations base their demands on the untested assumption that the only way to accelerate production is to work longer hours. I had a rare opportunity to explore this assumption. First, I studied individuals' use of time at work and the effects on them, their families, and the corporation. Then, I was able to alter the collective use of time among the group members I studied and compare the effects of the change on them and their corporation. This opportunity enabled me to explore whether there might be a way of working that achieves marketplace success for the corporation without requiring extreme personal and familial sacrifices from employees.

Research at Ditto

I studied product development engineers at Ditto, a Fortune 500 corporation. These engineers face immense pressure to get their product to market as soon as possible. Statistics show substantial losses in profit when products are delivered to market even slightly behind schedule. Product development engineers are therefore expected to sacrifice their lives outside of work for the company, and ultimately for their own careers. In this environment, where long hours of work are assumed to be critical to the product's success, I examined what individuals are actually doing at work and whether, from the organization's perspective, this use of time is optimal for achieving the organization's goals.

The engineers I studied were developing PEARL, a color laser printer. I had been involved in research in this particular division at Ditto for close to two years. When funding was committed to PEARL, I moved nearby in order to observe full-time a product's development from the commitment of funding until its launch. The majority of my observations come from this nine-month period, although I continued to follow this team after my intense stay for another two years. In total, I spent over four years studying the work of Ditto engineers.

Since my purpose was to explore individuals' use of time and the implications for themselves, their families, and their corporation, I observed engineers' daily routines at work—in front of the computer, in labs, in meetings, and at lunches. Initially, I interviewed the members of the team to gather background information. I "shadowed" engineers, following them around to observe everything they did and writing down each activity as it occurred. Shadowing group members provided me with an in-depth understanding of how they spend their time at work and what is involved in each type of activity.

I also wanted detailed data from many individuals on multiple occasions. So I asked engineers to keep their own logs of what they did all day. On randomly chosen days I asked three or four engineers to wear a digital watch that beeped on the hour, and at each beep to write down everything that they had done during the previous hour. I followed each tracking day with a debriefing interview in which I asked the engineers to talk through their log sheets, reviewing for me all their activities.

Since I also wanted to document the effects of work on family members, I went to the homes of the married engineers and interviewed their spouses. When possible, I also shared a meal with the family and conducted an additional interview with both spouses.

Finally, I engaged the engineers in a collaborative field experiment that explored the benefits of altering their use of time at work. This experiment is discussed in Chapter 10. Refer to the Methodological Appendix for a more extensive discussion of my data collection and analysis.

Overview of the Book

The purpose of this book is to explore the way individuals currently use time at work and the potential benefits of change. I organize these topics into three parts, each of which begins with in-depth stories about specific engineers and then follows with more analytic chapters.

In Part I, I describe what is expected of engineers at Ditto. I document the importance engineers ascribe to doing high-visibility work, always being willing to accommodate the demands of the work, and putting in long hours. Part I concludes in Chapter 4 with a discussion of the effects of these expectations on the engineers and their families.

Part II homes in on the specifics of how engineers actually use time at work. I describe the lack of helping, the constant interruptions, and the crisis mentality. Part II concludes in Chapter 8 with a discussion of the negative effects of the way of using time on *the product's development*.

In Part III, I explore the possibility of change. I describe one individual's negative experience when she tried to take advantage of a flexible work option, and I also document a more successful collaborative experiment in which engineers collectively created blocks of "quiet time" when they could work uninterrupted. The managers credited this change for the product's on-time launch. Part III concludes in Chapter 11 with a discussion of the potential benefits of new work practices for the corporation, individuals, and their families.

Throughout the book, it is important to keep in mind that I am painting a picture of life as the engineers described it to me. I spoke to some managers and include their responses where appropriate, but I do not dwell on the managers' perspectives. It turns out, however, that understanding the engineers' world from their perspective leads to powerful insights about work and possibilities for change. The collaborative experiment reported in Chapter 10 and the managers' reaction to it validate the claim that engineers can improve their own personal lives as well as corporate productivity.

PART I

Life in the Fast Lane

Driving down Route 401 about twenty minutes from downtown, one could easily miss the Ditto site I studied. Those who know to exit and make a left under the underpass, however, find a large complex. Ditto has nearly 100,000 employees worldwide and 3,000 of them work at this site, Ditto's primary facility for design and manufacturing.

From the outside, the complex looks like a cluster of long, white, single-story warehouses. It is not an easy site for strangers to navigate. None of the buildings have distinguishing features, or even names, only numbers. After passing three long warehouses and several parking lots, one approaches Building 113 on the left.

The building effectively excludes the outside world. It is dimly lit and has no windows. Only at the front entrance or the only other one, at the back, is it possible to see whether it is day or night, or whether the sun is shining or a terrible winter storm has hit. Time is oddly suspended in the vacuumlike atmosphere.

The interior of Building 113 is divided into many large open areas, each subdivided into cubicles, sometimes as many as fifty or a hundred in a "room." Engineers are each assigned a cubicle, and those of lower grade levels must share. Only after eight years at Ditto, or the equivalent level of experience, may an engineer occupy his or her own cubicle. Offices (with walls and doors for

privacy) are reserved for managers. In addition to clusters of cubicles, there are also labs scattered throughout the building. Labs
consist of open spaces filled with computers, printers, and other
machines used for testing. Often, labs also serve as unofficial stor-
age space, prompting thoughts of a garage that desperately needs
spring cleaning.

PEARL's product development team was housed in Building
113. Both Max and Laura were members of this team. Milton was
its product manager. He reported to Jim, one of sixteen division
vice-presidents, who reported to six business unit vice-presidents;
Jim reported to Kent. Jim's division was losing money. Both Kent
and Jim were concerned about the division's future, and they were
counting on PEARL to turn the division around.

PEARL was positioned to sell for $10,000. The goal was to in-
stall 4,630 units by the following year's end (six months after the
June launch date). PEARL's target market of smaller office groups
was completely new for this division, which formerly made much
larger electronic machines that sold for ten times the amount.
Management hoped that PEARL would not only prove profitable
but would also position Ditto in this new market. There were plans
to follow it with an entire product family. If PEARL did not succeed, the rest of the plans would be worthless. Two competitor
products had already been launched. The team knew about one,
but the announcement of the second was completely unexpected.

Engineers at Ditto typically take three, four, or sometimes five
years to develop a product. Most of the engineers who worked on
PEARL were most recently involved in RUBY, a product that took
five years to design. Suddenly, with PEARL, they faced the daunt-
ing task of developing a product in nine months.

Magnifying the challenge of PEARL's time frame was the
newness of the technology involved in its creation. The technology differed radically from the type with which many of the engineers were familiar, and the engineers involved lacked many of
the basic skills necessary to do their work. Limited time and
money prevented the engineers from acquiring the initial training
they needed. They were, therefore, forced to learn on the job, and
their daily confrontations with a steep learning curve slowed their
productivity.

Software Group

For the nine months from commitment of funding until product launch, the PEARL product development team consisted of forty-five individuals. The team included Milton, the product manager, and his staff of eight managers (see Figure 1).[1]

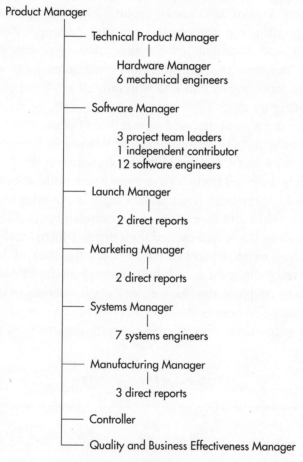

Product Manager

— Technical Product Manager
  |
  Hardware Manager
  6 mechanical engineers

— Software Manager
  |
  3 project team leaders
  1 independent contributor
  12 software engineers

— Launch Manager
  |
  2 direct reports

— Marketing Manager
  |
  2 direct reports

— Systems Manager
  |
  7 systems engineers

— Manufacturing Manager
  |
  3 direct reports

— Controller

— Quality and Business Effectiveness Manager

FIGURE 1
Organization chart for PEARL project

---

[1] From September 1993 until January 1994, the software manager reported directly to Carl, the senior software manager, and only indirectly to Milton, the product manager. Carl and Milton both reported to Jim, the division vice president.

I focused my research, in particular, on the software manager and the sixteen individuals who reported to him. I wanted to understand in detail how people use time both individually and collectively, and this group was small enough that I could study all its members, yet large enough that I could study its three subgroups as well as the group as a whole. Each subgroup of four engineers reported to a project team leader, whose name was used to identify the subgroup. For example, the four engineers reporting to Laura were known as "Laura's group." The three project team leaders, in turn, reported to the software manager, Zeth, who ultimately had responsibility for the software development of PEARL. There was also one individual contributor, John, who had no people reporting to him and who himself reported directly to Zeth (see Figure 2).

Group members possessed a great deal of education and experience. At the time of commitment to funding in September, no one had been employed by Ditto for less than three and a half years. All had earned bachelor's degrees in scientific and engineering fields. Half the team had master's degrees in computer science or related fields, and four more were enrolled in part-time master's programs. Most had earned their degrees from local schools.

The first two chapters in Part I detail the lives of Max and Laura, two of the most successful engineers on the PEARL team. Max's story depicts the life of an "organizational superstar." Laura's story illuminates the tradeoffs one must continually make between succeeding at work and devoting time to family life. In

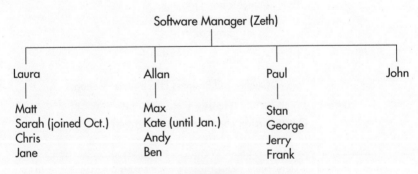

FIGURE 2
Organization chart for software team

Chapter 3, I step back from these individual cases to describe in more general terms the engineers' perception of the criteria for succeeding at work and the costs of not conforming. Chapter 4 concludes Part I with an exploration of the effects of the work demands on life at home.

1

Organizational Superstar: Max's Story

When I first met Max in September, he told me that I would need some background to understand his approach to work. He explained, "For the eight months prior to June of last year, I was working 80- to 90-hour weeks continuously. I took July off, and now I am back, onto my next assignment." He was now "in lazy mode," he said. "I have proved myself. Management knows that they can count on me when they need me. . . . currently my work is under control, and I intend to take it easy for a while. When there is work to be done, then I will do it. Now, there is not much." Max was working a sixty-hour week at this time. He had enrolled in school to work on his master's in computer science. In order to attend classes he had to leave work every Tuesday and Thursday by four-thirty. Asked to elaborate on his notion of "lazy mode," Max explained, "I am burned out." Nonetheless, he said, "I will be back at it as soon as I have more to do. No one around here can afford to be lazy for too long. There is too little job security."

Max made work his top priority. Moreover, he believed that everyone should be as willing as he to accommodate work crises. He said, "It is not the company's job to manage crises. It is the individual's responsibility to accommodate." Max found it particularly irritating when people complain about not getting paid overtime. He always reminded them, "At least you have a job."

A Day in the Life of Max

One Thursday in mid-November, I asked Max to keep track of everything he did the next day, from the time he woke up in the morning until he went to bed at night. The following Monday morning we discussed the day as he recorded it.

6:14	I woke up.
6:20–6:40	I got ready for work.
6:40	I left for work.
7:10	I arrived at work.
7:10–7:20	I went to my desk, took off my coat, checked my e-mail.
7:20–7:28	I headed to the lab, but I ran into my manager. We went together to get coffee. I statused him [reported his progress].
7:28–7:35	We went back to the lab. I finished statusing my manager. At the same time, I set up the printer.
7:35	My manager went to work at his computer (also in the lab). I began my own work.
7:35–8:30	I worked on my code.
8:30–8:43	I interrupted Andy and asked him a few questions about some common code. That reminded Andy that he had changed some other stuff about which he had forgotten to tell me. We discussed the changes.
8:43–9:00	I worked on my code.
9:00–9:03	Andy had a few questions about his code.
9:03–9:40	I worked on my code.
9:40–9:45	My manager needed more status information for the report he was filling out.
9:45–11:00	I worked on my code.
11:00–11:30	My computer went down. I went to find the system expert, who came to the lab and fixed the problem. I went back to work. But now I had a different problem, and I did not know what the source was. (It was not until the afternoon that I

	found out that the system expert had introduced the new problem when he fixed my original problem.)
11:30–12:30	The problem remained unsolved, but two engineers came by for lunch. A group of us went to McDonald's.
12:30–1:00	I came back to the lab. Now, another engineer was having the same problem. It was then that we realized that it was a system problem that had been introduced by the system expert earlier in the day. We went to find him.
1:00	Zeth stopped by to tell us that there was a one o'clock meeting on planning the integration among the software teams, and we should all attend.
1:10–1:45	I went to the meeting. (It should have involved only the project team leaders. There was no reason for all the engineers to be there.)
1:45–2:30	I worked on my code.
2:30–2:40	Ben was having a problem, and so I tried to show him how to do it.
2:40–4:00	I worked on my code.
4:00–6:30	I worked with Ben, helping him to make his code integrate with mine. (Ben is slow. I know a lot more than he does. It is quicker for me to just do it rather than wait around for him to struggle through.)
6:30–6:33	Another engineer stopped by to see if we wanted to go out for "happy hour." I didn't, but we called it quits. I went home.
7:00	I arrived home. I was waiting for a phone call from my girlfriend.
7:00–9:00	I ate dinner, watched some TV, and played music.
9:00–10:00	My girlfriend called, and we talked.
10:00	I went to bed.

According to Max, this was not a typical day because there were fewer interruptions from his managers than usual. Max said, "It was a much less active day than most during the past few weeks. . . . It was much more productive than usual; that should tell you something." In terms of the time after work, Max said it was a typical Friday evening. When I asked if he would have liked to have left earlier because it was a Friday, he responded, "Not really. I don't have much to do at home at night."

Max's log captures the basic temporal structure of the engineer's day. Engineers tend to arrive at Ditto between seven and nine in the morning and leave between five and seven in the evening, unless they must stay late to resolve a crisis. Typically, they have a meeting of some sort to attend and spend the rest of the day writing code. Interruptions, however, are common. Engineers prefer long interruptions that have been planned in advance to more frequent, spontaneous ones. Yet, as Max's day exemplifies, interruptions are typically short, numerous and (more or less) spontaneous.

On this day, Max went out for lunch. Typically, he ate in the cafeteria at work. Not all engineers take a lunch break. There does not seem to be a direct relationship between the success of an engineer and a pattern of skipping lunch. If anything, the relationship is the reverse of what one might expect. Many of the most successful engineers do go to lunch. Skipping lunch often indicates that the individual perceives actual work time limited and uses the lunch period to get some extra work done. In general, however, there is more reward and recognition if one stays an hour later in the evening than if one skips lunch. When one moves up in the organization this pattern changes. None of the project team leaders or managers take time for lunch on a regular basis. They work through lunch and for the extra hours at the end of the day as well.

Individualistic Approach to Work

While at work, Max focused first and foremost on his code, his individual deliverables. He responded to requests from others for help on their code by advising on how something should be done or by taking over the problem and solving it himself. When Max helped others, he drew attention to the fact that he was providing them support. The person seeking help was often made to feel inadequate. Max provided neither the type of "behind the scenes" help nor the instinctive teaching that will later be described in the case of Matt. As one engineer put it, "Max has a way of making me feel slow and inadequate, no matter what I do. He is always putting me down, criticizing my pace and questioning my attack of problems."

Even when giving help might have benefited his own code, Max was often unwilling to focus on someone else's needs. One day Stan, who had been assigned to help Max, wanted to spend some time reviewing what each was working on in order to avoid duplication of effort. Max agreed to listen to Stan but insisted on simultaneously trying to solve a different problem on his computer. Because his concentration was elsewhere, Max took several minutes to respond to each of Stan's questions. Stan, consequently, had to stand around in the lab for over half an hour just to get Max to respond to five minutes worth of questions. Once Stan finally left the lab, Max said to me, "Stan is too slow. . . . He does not give me the information I need quickly enough." Yet, Max's unwillingness to focus on the conversation with Stan made his assessment a self-fulfilling prophecy.

If Max did not consider a colleague his peer in intelligence, speed, and commitment, he believed working with that person was a waste of his time. He would rather do it himself. Few of Max's colleagues met his exacting standards. On his last product, Max worked on a team with two other engineers. One was an intelligent, overly committed workaholic whom Max respected. The other engineer, in Max's opinion, did not measure up. She was willing to work "only" fifty- or sixty-hour weeks, not the eighty or ninety hours Max and his buddy put in. Eventually, she left the group, enabling Max and his buddy to continue at their own intense pace. In the end management considered them heroes because they accomplished the task with less labor than originally allocated.

Max's lack of concern for others, their work, or the product as a whole rendered him a threat to the technical success of the product. An engineer summed up the group consensus about Max when he described him as "an expert in solving problems, but a terror in the process." Max was among the most likely to find a solution to a technical problem, but he also might create troubling side effects in the process because he tended to focus on his own work and not the implications for others' work. When one is attempting to solve a software problem, it is easy to create another problem in the process and not discover it until much later. Because all the code is interdependent, one engineer's function may operate well but affect someone else's code negatively. Yet, no one may be aware that the code exerts this adverse effect. As one engineer noted, "It is easy to recognize when things do not work because they blow up in your face, but it is more difficult to know when good work is occurring. Only in retrospect, if nothing blew up, can you recognize the work was good. But as it is going on, you cannot tell good work, only bad work."

The larger organization may suffer as a consequence of Max's work style. Still, Max was generously rewarded for long hours, apparent commitment, and obvious technical capability. The previous year he received the top raise in his group and additional financial bonuses for "outstanding" performance.[1] These rewards support the perspective shared by the engineers that what the managers evaluate is whether they do whatever it takes to complete their individual deliverables.

Life Outside of Work

Max, thirty years old and single, lived with several roommates. He had been dating his girlfriend "on again, off again" for over two years. He said he was very committed to making their relationship work. In the middle of the year, Max bought his girlfriend a gift that cost over ten thousand dollars. He told no one at work be-

---

[1] Each year in February, the engineers receive performance evaluations based on the previous January through December. This year, the top 10 percent of engineers were awarded a 6 percent increase in salary. Max was in this category. He was also awarded several thousand dollars for his long hours and individual accomplishments during the spring prior to my arrival when he was working eighty- to ninety-hour weeks.

cause, as he explained in an interview, "people around here will laugh." Max said, "It is things like this investment that have enabled me to win her over. . . . I am in love with her, and so I do weird things. I didn't have the money to buy [the present]; so I had to borrow it."

Despite his financial commitment to his girlfriend, Max expressed doubts about their relationship. He complained: "She is very intelligent, but she does not know how to cook and clean. . . . She is the baby in her family. . . . She does not know how to take care of herself, her family, or her home. She is used to everyone taking care of her." He was also concerned that she was not supportive of his work: "She says I am too ambitious. She thinks I should work less hard. . . . She doesn't understand me."

Max and his girlfriend saw each other over the weekends; that was all the time Max felt he could spend with her. He devoted the majority of his time to achieving the work goals he had set for himself. He conveyed uncertainty about staying at Ditto and progressing into management. He talked instead about starting his own entrepreneurial venture:

> I am interested in doing everything, and I will do whatever I do best. I believe that there is no limit to one's potential. I will continue to take advantage of the opportunities at Ditto, and if management is a path that is offered, I will certainly do it. But, I am not sure I want to spend my whole life here. I am not satisfied with my life. I feel like I do not reach out for new opportunities. I just go along, never taking control over my life and my career. . . . Many people complain instead of just doing. I think that in order to make the world a better place, you have to do it yourself. You cannot count on anyone but yourself.

While this individualistic and determined approach to work left little time for his girlfriend, it made Max extremely successful at Ditto. In the next chapter, I describe the approach of another successful Ditto employee, who juggles more substantial demands from her life outside of work on top of her career. Unlike Max, Laura is married and has three young children. She experiences the conflict that results when one has an intense desire to succeed at work and yet cannot make work one's first priority at all times.

2

Ideal Female Employee: Laura's Story

Laura usually did not get to work until eight-thirty, after she dropped her children, ages seven, two, and one, off at day care. She had to leave by five-thirty because the day care center closed at six. As it was, Laura was often the last one to pick up her children. She said, "It is common for them to be shutting off the lights and locking the doors as I come running in." Still, Laura managed to stay on top of her deliverables.

A Day in the Life of Laura

As with Max, I asked Laura to track her activities during the course of a randomly selected day, by coincidence also a Friday. When we discussed her day the following Monday, she reported:

12:45 A.M.	I woke up in my two-year-old's bed. I went into my own bed.
3:30	My two-year-old crawled into my bed.
4:00	The alarm went off because my husband was going to work early.
4:00–4:45	I was up while my husband got ready for work. (He turns on all the lights while he gets dressed.)

6:10	I woke up. (For me that is severely oversleeping. Usually I get up at 5:30)
6:10–6:20	I showered.
6:20–7:00	I ate breakfast, made lunches, laid out clothes, got partially dressed. (I get ready in stages of 5–10 minutes.)
7:00	My mom left for work. (My mother has lived with us for the past two years.)
7:00–7:30	I got the baby and my seven-year-old up and dressed and fed them breakfast.
7:30–7:50	I finished getting ready, straightened up the house, and did the dishes. (The two boys were watching TV.)
7:50–8:05	I woke up my two-year-old, got him dressed and fed.
8:05–8:15	I got the kids' coats on and got them into the car.
8:20–8:35	I got to day care and spent a few minutes getting the kids settled and talked to their teachers.
8:50	I arrived at work. (Very late.) Zeth and Andy saw me and grabbed me. I didn't even get in the door before the first hallway conversation began.
8:50–9:00	I talked with Zeth and Andy in the hall. (It was good because I'd had this piece of information in my head that I had not shared with anyone, so I got the chance to share it. I disliked the conversation though because I still hadn't had a chance to take off my coat.)
9:00–9:20	I delivered software to the applications lab. No one was there, so I didn't leave it. Instead, I wandered around looking for someone to give it to.
9:20	I gave it to Dan so I wouldn't have to redeliver it.
9:25	I interrupted Jane and asked her how things were going.
9:30	I started to work on what was supposed to be my big task for the day—my progress report—which I thought I could get done in the morning. (In the afternoon I was planning to work on a presentation. I never got to the presentation, and I ended

	up finishing my progress report over the week-end.)
9:45	Zeth and Chip stopped by, and we started talking about a demo for Monday. We decided to meet at four that afternoon to prepare. (That changed my plans for the afternoon. Not only did I have to meet them at four, but I had to do some preparation first.)
10:00	I went back to working on my progress report. (This is the weekly status report that is due on Wednesday, but I was late.)
10:25	Chris came in, and we talked about his status.
10:45	I went back to work on my progress report.
11:05	Roy stopped by to discuss the user interface.
11:17	I started work on my progress report again.
11:30–11:50	Paul stopped by to report on feedback from a meeting he had attended on my behalf.
11:50	I left Ditto and ran an errand during lunch. (I needed something to wear for Thanksgiving dinner, and I knew this was my only chance. It is rare for me to leave work during the day.)
1:00	I returned from the mall and talked to Jane and Chris about the demo plans for the 4 o'clock meeting. I planned to meet with Chris in the lab at two-fifteen.
1:30	I went back to work on my progress report.
2:18	I went to the lab to work on the demo with Chris.
3:00	I reviewed my progress report with Zeth. (Zeth questioned it. He said, "Is this number right? Is that number right? Are you positive?" He requested some changes because he wanted it to paint a rosier picture than it did.)
3:10	I went back to work on my progress report.
3:16	Eric stopped by to talk about a nondisclosure agreement.
3:20	I went back to work on my progress report.
3:30	Jane stopped by with problems on the demo code.
3:40	I went back to work on my progress report.

4:00	I worked on the demo with John. Zeth stopped by in the middle to see how we were doing.
5:23	I left work. (The demo wasn't working when I left, and it was scheduled for eight to ten o'clock on Monday morning. Chip told me on Monday that he was on the couch Sunday night with his feet up watching football when he felt so bad for Zeth and this demo that he came to work at 4 A.M. on Monday. I came at 6 A.M. We got the demo working for the 8 A.M. meeting.)
5:40	I picked up the kids at day care
6:00	I returned home and ordered pizza. (Friday night is pizza night. Typically my husband picks up the kids and gets the pizza, but on this particular day he wanted to go to "happy hour" with his friends from school; so I picked them up.)
6:45	After dinner, I gave the baby a bath. I took my son to a friend's to spend the night.
7:00–9:00	I played with the other two kids, and then put the baby to bed.
9:00	My husband came home and he watched our two-year-old, while I wallpapered until eleven.
11:10	I showered and went to bed.
12:10	The phone rang. My son wasn't feeling well at the sleepover and wanted to come home. I went to get him.
12:30	I finally went to bed for the night.

After reviewing her day, Laura said: "The fact that it took me a whole day to get my progress report done is not right. I don't envision that as a big task. It is not a big task. What they're asking is very reasonable, which should only take a few minutes to put together. But any task I would have tried to do on Friday would have taken an entire day because of all the interruptions." She then added, "But all these interruptions are very typical."

There are two main differences between a usual day for Laura and a usual day for Max. First, because Laura was a first-line manager and Max a senior engineer, Laura had fewer deliverables of her own to worry about than Max, but she also had more responsibility for making sure that the four engineers she managed completed their work. Second, Max had set up his life in such a way that he could easily accommodate the demands of his work, whereas Laura had more demands on her time outside of work which she felt responsible to satisfy. It is the latter difference on which I focus in this chapter.

Work-Family Issues

Laura did not feel she had the option of making an open-ended commitment to work. Her husband also worked at Ditto, in a different division at a level equivalent to her boss, the software manager. Laura explained that her husband was the one who oversaw the details around the house: "He organizes the lawn service; he hires the maid; he pays the bills; he calls the dentist; he does the weekly shopping. He is the administrator. . . . I take care of the children; I do the cleaning beyond the maid; I pick up; I cook; I do laundry, gardening, ironing and the shopping, besides the weekly grocery shopping."

Laura said her husband worked longer hours than she did. If he did get involved in transporting the children to day care, he preferred to drop them off in the morning, so he had flexibility at night. He usually came home between six-thirty and seven, just as Laura was serving dinner. She said they quibbled a lot over whose work meetings were more important and who should have to skip out to care for the kids, but ultimately, her husband said, "if there is ever a real question, my work wins out."

When one of their children was sick, it was Laura who usually stayed home. She gave an example of a recent work day when her son woke up with an ear infection. Her husband had been at work since two o'clock that morning.

> The thought crossed my mind that since he had already worked a full day, from two in the morning until eight in the morning, he might be willing to come home. But he never offered and I never mentioned it. . . . I don't really mind, because I have

maternal feelings about wanting to be with my kids when they are sick. I want to make sure that I ask the doctor all the right questions. . . . whenever the kids are sick or hurt, they always come to me first. If they are well, they like their father as much. . . . My two-year-old wakes up in the middle of the night, and he always yells, "Mommy." Only if I wait long enough will he ever yell, "Daddy." And only then can I roll over in bed and make my husband go care for him.

As if Laura's responsibilities for her work, her three kids, and her husband were not enough, her mother, who had been divorced since Laura was a child, had also lived with them for the past two years while she recovered from a serious illness. According to Laura, her mother was not much help around the house or with the children: "My mother hates to get the kids ready for school and drop them off or pick them up and prepare dinner. She finds that all too stressful."

Accommodating Work Demands

Laura took on much of the responsibility at home, but sometimes her work made her unavailable at home. One day, Laura was so busy she did not check her voice mail all day. At 5:15 P.M., she found that she had seven messages. The first one went back to 11:20 that morning, when the school nurse had called to tell her that her eldest son was sick and needed to be picked up from school. The second message, at noon, was her husband saying that he had picked up their son, but he had a meeting at three o'clock and she had better come home. At one o'clock, he left the same message, and again at two. At three o'clock there was another message from her husband saying he had taken their son to a neighbor's house and was now on his way to work. At four o'clock her husband left a message saying that he needed her to help him pick up the car at the garage. At five there was a message from her husband saying, "Forget it, forget it, forget it all." When Laura got home that night, she reported, "My husband was livid. He thought that I had intentionally been ignoring him. I told him I would not do that. . . . In retrospect I am glad I never heard those messages because my son was not really sick. He just wanted attention, and I had a ton of work to do."

Laura's success at work derives at least in part from her willingness to accommodate to work despite her family responsibilities. Managers hold up Laura as a "model *female* employee." More than once, I heard a Ditto manager turn to an employee and ask why she could not be more like Laura. "Look at Laura," a manager would say, "she has a husband and three kids, and yet she still is able to do it all."

Laura did not regularly come in early or stay late unless there was an extremely pressing issue, or she was specifically asked to do so by a manager. Nonetheless, she put in considerable extra time in other ways. One day a week, Laura tried to be at the office by two o'clock in the morning to catch up on the work that she was not able to do during business hours. She would work straight through the day until five-thirty. Laura used to do this work at the dining room table, until she ran into her manager in the middle of the night and found that he "was really impressed. . . . I used to just go to the kitchen table and use my PC, but after the reaction I got from my manager I decided it was important to do that early morning work in the office. . . . It is better to be seen here if you are going to work in the middle of the night."

Laura fit in extra work time in other ways as well. One weekend in the spring, for example, she had to get some work done, but she did not want to leave her husband at home with the children because he would be resentful. She played outdoors with the kids Saturday morning and afternoon, fed them dinner, bathed them, and put them to bed. Once the kids were asleep and "my husband sat happily in front of the TV watching a hockey game" Laura felt she could go to work. It was about eight o'clock. She worked through the night and said she felt good about the work since she had accomplished it without "sacrificing . . . her family."

In another case, during a two-week period last year when her husband was away, Laura was assigned a short-term, high-visibility project, which demanded extraordinary hours. For two straight weeks, she would leave work every evening at five-thirty, pick up the kids from day care, feed them, play with them, and put them to bed. She said she would then take a short nap and get up around midnight to start the next day's work. She worked at home until five and then got the kids up, dressed, fed, and off to day care before coming into the office to work until five-thirty in the afternoon. She kept to this schedule for two weeks, never mentioning to her manager that her husband was away.

In the end, Laura always seemed to get her work done, and her work was well received. The year I was on site she was awarded a lump-sum bonus given to the top 10 percent of managers.[1] Moreover, in the past five years, Laura received four promotions. Last year she got a double promotion. As a result, Laura was higher in grade level than most of her same-age peers. She earned less money than colleagues at her grade level, however, because pay increases are based only partly on grade level and partly on time spent at each grade level. Since Laura was promoted so quickly, she did not have time to accumulate incremental salary increases. She therefore received a relatively low salary for an individual with her level of responsibility.

Laura was "handpicked" for the company's employee development program. She received unique opportunities both for improving her skill set and for gaining visibility from senior management. For two and a half days during the fall, Laura was taken off-site to a workshop that included several training sessions and a dinner with Ditto's CEO.

Because Laura is a woman, she can do things that men at her level cannot do. No one raises an eyebrow when Laura leaves a meeting at five-thirty to pick up her children from day care. When a man does the same thing, skeptical comments are made. One day Laura mentioned to a male peer (who also has a young son) that she has privileges he does not. He responded, "I recognize that." Laura then expressed concern, "It is not fair, I know, but what can I do?" Her colleague just shook his head and said, "I don't know, but someone has to pick up the kids. I just wish I could too."

Laura may have high visibility and accelerated opportunities because she is a woman. She may receive "special" treatment at

---

[1] Because of the company layoffs in January, it was decided that managers would not receive a raise this year, but the top 10 percent received a one-time 10 percent lump-sum award.

work because she is a woman. Nevertheless, she is a dedicated worker willing to do everything humanly possible to accommodate to the demands of her work.

Reflecting on Life

From a distance, Laura may appear to have it all. She is married to her high school sweetheart, also a very successful Ditto employee. They live in one of the most expensive homes I visited, in an upper-middle-class suburb some twenty minutes from the office. They could afford day care for all three children, house cleaning once a week, and exotic vacations once or twice a year. Moreover, managers were constantly pointing to Laura as a role model. From their perspective, she demonstrated that women can "do it all."

Laura, however, did not feel that her life was ideal. Whenever I told her that she portrayed this image she became visibly upset and reminded me that she was "tormented" by all the demands she had to try to satisfy. Laura believed that it was only a manufactured image that things were "in control" in her life. She was very concerned that she was not able to do anything to the level she would like. She felt that she was not performing well enough at work and that her children would be better off if she did not work. She said: "I am not happy with my day-to-day life. I would like to be more organized at work and have more quantity time with the family, but the two are at the expense of each other."

Laura thought that her children were deprived of parental attention. They lacked what she referred to as "quantity time"; she felt that "quality time" was not enough. She believed that her kids needed more actual time with her. She described one domestic scene to a group of fellow software engineers: "My children are so naughty in the summer. The other day, I walked into the kitchen and my two-year-old yelled, 'Mommy, Mommy look what I am doing.' He was spitting juice through a straw all over the kitchen wall. Grape juice was dripping everywhere." One of the female engineers listening exclaimed, "Laura, that child is starved for attention." Laura muttered, "I just wonder what I am doing to my kids," and then fell silent.

Yet, at the same time, Laura felt constant pressure to keep achieving. She said, "I know that I am a woman being set up for success. I am given lots of opportunities, but in return I must continually live up to their expectations." Her manager recently informed her that she had to do something next year, either go back to school or take a more visible position as the product manager's (her boss's boss) "right hand man." She must show progress and not settle into any role if she was to continue ascending the hierarchy. Despite her desire to spend more time with her children, Laura therefore enrolled in an MBA program for the fall, planning to take two master's-level courses per semester.

Laura seemed quite conflicted, if not confused. One moment she told me her family was her first priority, and the next she described her ambitious career aspirations. At one point she said, "In the long term I want to be a division vice-president. I want to continue succeeding, getting more promotions and more responsibility." The next moment she flipped back to her family orientation: "But I know I cannot handle any more responsibility, especially if I start school this fall." Then she flipped again: "I can never do the same job twice. That would be a sign of failure to me. It would not be continual movement upward like I am used to. I do not feel like I can cut back when I am in school. I cannot expect to finish school and instantly be handed some great job just because I have a degree. I have to continue to climb when I am in school." Thus, the same woman who wants to take more time for her children will probably never do so because she is afraid of ruining her career opportunities. Laura struggles because she wants to be a star at work and a star at home.

The stories of Max and Laura illuminate the key components the engineers perceive to be necessary for success at Ditto, and the effects of these demands on their lives outside of work. In the next chapter, I elaborate in more detail the criteria of success and the price of nonconformity.

3

Individual Heroics:
Criteria for Success

According to the engineers, reward and recognition depend on completion of individual deliverables. Even though the product's development requires successful integration of all the code, engineers perceive their own deliverables as most important.[1] One engineer explained:

> I have three high-priority items on my to-do list. I know that one of them is the most pressing for the company, but the other two come from my boss. I will do those two first because that is in my best interest. Maybe if there was a way to have peer evaluations as well as manager evaluations we would be encouraged to act in the best interest of each other and not just do what our managers tell us to do. Maybe then we would make better decisions for the company as to how we prioritize our work. But currently, that is not the way it is.

Because of their understanding of the existing organizational reward system, if faced with the choice of getting a product out the proverbial door or making sure that their own deliverables

---

[1] The perception that one's own work is most important reaches far beyond these engineers. In the 1830s, the French philosopher, Alexis de Tocqueville was one of the first to single out the importance of individualism in America. More recently, Robert Bellah and his colleagues (1985) have found that individualism remains a cornerstone of American society.

are perfect, few engineers would opt for the timely product launch. According to one engineer, "When the management launched RUBY [an earlier product], there was a bug in my code. They still made the decision to launch it. They felt it wasn't worth the time to fix the problem. For me, I will always have to live with the tarnished image. I will always be identified with the flaw in that product. Since then, I try never to release my code without checking for all the bugs first, even if it holds them up." Engineers perceive that their reputations depend on successful completion of their individual deliverables, not on the product's profitability.

Criteria for Recognition

According to the engineers, success requires not only that they complete their own code but that their code be considered "high visibility." They explain that "accommodating the demands of the work" is also critical. Furthermore, the engineers believe that simply "being present" is necessary. Below I elaborate on each of these criteria perceived by engineers as determinants of individual success at work.[2]

What engineers mean by "high-visibility" work is output that managers consider crucial to their own success. High-visibility projects bring engineers to the attention of managers, and stellar accomplishments on these projects bring positive recognition. One engineer summed it up: "I want visibility. Visibility is critical to move up in this company. . . . My work is not providing me an opportunity to shine. I don't want to be in the background any more." The professional "risk" of working on a high-visibility project, however, is that any "failures" are thought to be potentially quite damaging to one's progress.

---

[2] Robert Jackall's (1988) study of managers supports the Ditto engineers' belief that success at work depends at least as much on the perception that one is a "rising star" as it does on one's actual work output. Jackall writes, "Unquestionably, 'hitting your numbers'—that is, meeting the profit commitments . . .—is important, but only within the social context. . . . Profits matter, but it is much more important in the long run to be perceived as 'promotable' " (p. 62).

High-visibility work is vital not just for individual recognition but also to ensure access to the resources needed to accomplish one's work. As one project team leader explained:

> My team's work is less critical to the project, and therefore we get much less attention. This is good because it enables us to work along at our own pace, but we lack that extra push. We can never get the resources we need. It makes it all the harder to succeed. . . . Management will pay attention if we succeed in the end. But that makes it nearly impossible to shine. It is all or nothing. We have no visibility along the way. And we lack the support to make sure that we'll make it in the end.

It is more likely that one will succeed if one is in a visible position. Yet to be assigned high visibility work, one must have a record of success. One engineer articulated his perception of this cycle: "I expect to get another promotion this year. . . . my perception is that they perceive me as a top performer in the group. . . . They keep putting me in very high-visibility, high-pressure positions."

Beyond successfully performing high-visibility work, engineers believe that they must be perceived as always willing to "accommodate the demands of the work." One engineer commented, "I never disagree, although sometimes I complain later on. But when I am first told, I always agree. I am the employee, and I am supposed to agree." Moreover, engineers believe they should be willing to do whatever is asked, not just in terms of producing output but also in terms of working whatever hours are deemed necessary to get the job done. The work follows no predictable schedule. Demands often arise at the last minute. For example, a crisis might result from a bug that is delaying release or a problem with the printer in the testing lab or the need for a "work-around"—a temporary, Band-Aid solution—so a functioning product can be demonstrated. Whatever the cause, crises require immediate response.

One evening the software manager called one of his engineers at home to find out what time the engineer would be in the next morning. The engineer recounted:

> I would not have gone in until probably close to 9 A.M., but after Zeth called I made sure to be there by 7 A.M. What he said to me

last night was: "I want to make sure we have our release ready for Sunrise [a daily meeting to review the team's progress] in the morning," which is at eight-thirty, "because I want to be able to go in and say, 'You're wrong. We have our release ready.'" Zeth always assumes that everything is going to go okay. And nothing ever goes perfectly smoothly, especially when you try to rush something and get it done really quick. Then you always fuck it up and have to do it again. I don't think he realizes that. So he just assumed that if I came in real early and gave the code to John, and he made the proms, and we plugged them into the machine, and then they would be ready to go, and he could go to Sunrise at eight-thirty and say, "Here's the release." But it turns out that we didn't have it working until when? Eleven-thirty or something like that. I knew it would never be ready by eight-thirty. That would have taken a miracle.

This engineer, however, never mentioned his well-founded doubts to his manager. Rather, he simply agreed to arrive early and give his best effort. Such willingness to be present and to work diligently, whether or not one thinks the task is feasible, is thought to be a critical part of how one's final output is evaluated.

Accommodating work is believed to be particularly crucial around key dates when software is supposed to be released. Taking the date seriously signifies commitment to the team. One day Sarah came to work quite sick. She was sitting staring at her computer screen, unable to work. I asked her why she had come in. She said, "It is a major release date, and even though I know full well that the team will not be done, nor will I ever finish, I came in to signify to Laura [her project team leader] that I take this date seriously."

Willingness to accommodate work often involves giving up weekend and vacation plans. As one of the engineers explained, "You feel like a wimp telling people that you do not want to work Saturday, or you do not want to stay late at night. It is just something that you cannot do. You will always think twice before you say that around here." Another engineer explained, "You can only say no so many times. You need to think carefully before you say the word 'no,' and when you do, it had better be for a good reason."

Merely expressing a preference about what time a meeting should occur may be perceived by managers as signaling a lack of commitment. When the software manager mentioned a Saturday meeting, he assumed all would attend; he simply asked which four hours the group would prefer—morning or afternoon. One engineer spoke up, saying that he would prefer the afternoon. His manager joked, "Oh, you have baby-sitting responsibilities in the morning." The engineer was uncomfortable. "That is true," he said, but then quickly added, "Don't worry about my preference, I can easily hire a baby-sitter." The software manager then suggested that if the software group was first on the product manager's agenda they would be more likely to meet at the scheduled time rather than have to sit around all afternoon waiting their turn. The group agreed. The meeting was set for 8 A.M. The fact that at least one of the engineers would have to hire a baby-sitter was never mentioned again.

The engineers perceive that in order to be successful, they must always be available to work. Managers do not consider a late afternoon or Saturday meeting a serious infringement of engineers' time. Unless they are going away, engineers rarely voice discontent with such demands. Even long-planned trips (with nonrefundable tickets) may not constitute an acceptable excuse for missing a meeting, especially if managers perceive it as urgent (as they most often do).

One engineer left on a long-planned trip and flew back for two days in the midst of a one-week vacation, deserting his wife and two young children, in order to solve some problems in his code. Another planned a vacation several months in advance for the week following a major release. He had scheduled it purposely to accommodate the product development schedule. At the last minute, the schedule slipped, but he went on vacation anyway. His peers suspected that his decision to go would be held against him for a long time. As one project team leader said about another:

> Allan blew it today. He didn't cover for his engineer. He outright acknowledged that he was on vacation. Sure this is a long-standing vacation, and it would have been well planned if the schedule had not slipped, but now his work is the object of concern,

and he is not here. That doesn't look good. This will be in people's minds for a long time, and when promotions come around people will remember how he went on vacation before a major release.

The expectation is that if one is needed at work, one will be there. The work of software engineers at Ditto demands long hours. There always seems to be a crisis to resolve. It is not enough, however, to accommodate the demands of the work. Being physically present at odd times of the day and night is also thought to be critical to one's success. Others besides Laura show up very early because it impresses their managers. Some resort to tricks, leaving a coat in the office, say, or a car in the parking lot to give the appearance of "being present."

Even at the higher levels, one's physical presence is important. The senior software manager, Carl, explained his tactics for making sure that he is seen by his boss, the division vice-president. Carl said, "Jim leaves me a voice message very early most mornings, so I make a point to be here to pick up the phone when he calls. He is always impressed that I am in by 6 A.M."

Managers apparently interpret an engineer's extended presence as a positive contribution to the team's goals, not as an indication of an employee's inefficiency or inability to accomplish tasks within a normal workday. One engineer, for example, was having trouble completing some major deliverables. "If it weren't for the fact he was trying so hard," his manager said, "I think we would have lost faith in him a long time ago. But he works so hard, you just have to assume he must be working on something really challenging." Indeed, long hours are understood as a sign of commitment.

At the other extreme, not being present creates a bad impression. With ten days to go on a major software release, two of Allan's engineers stayed late, as did Allan's boss, Zeth. Even Zeth's boss at the time, Carl, stopped in as he was leaving work around six-thirty to check on the team's progress. Allan, however, left at six o'clock. His parents were visiting from out of town and a family gathering was planned. Allan felt that it was unnecessary for him to stay at work: "There was nothing that I could do to help. I lacked the technical expertise that was necessary. . . . So I left."

According to his engineers, Allan's departure presented no problem to the team: "There is nothing that he could have done to help out. . . . His presence would have been more of a hindrance than anything." Nor did the engineers feel that Zeth's presence was necessary: "He should have gone home too. It doesn't help us get the work done to have someone constantly standing over us. . . . We work best when we are left alone. . . . The managers just don't get it. They stand over us constantly, asking how they can be of help. All they are doing is distracting us. They can help the most by not trying to help at all."

Nevertheless, Carl, Zeth's manager, accosted Allan the next morning and asked why he had not stayed late the night before to support his engineers. Allan's response to the censure was not anger or defensiveness but guilt. He offered Carl an apology. He said to me, "I am such a schmuck. I should have stayed around and done busy work. It is terrible that I left. It looks really bad. . . . If I had stayed, Carl would have seen me here."

Being present has little to do with performance or substantive output. All the engineers felt there was no practical reason for Allan to have stayed late. In fact, his presence might have been a hindrance. Still, from Allan's (and, apparently, Carl's) perspective, leaving was a grave mistake. Allan feared that he had branded himself as uncommitted to the team. "I left them in a time of crisis," he said.

At the end of the calendar year, the managers meet in confidence to rank the software engineers. This list is not seen by anyone outside that room, but the ranking determines who receives what raises for the year.[3] The names of all of the software engineers in the division are listed, followed by a comment explaining

---

[3] The year I was on site, within each division, the top 10 percent of engineers received a 6 percent raise, the middle 70 percent received a 3 percent raise, and the bottom 20 percent received no raise. Of the twelve engineers I studied, two received a 6 percent raise, seven a 3 percent raise, and one got no raise. The remaining two engineers in my study were tied in ranking at the cutoff between a 6 percent and 3 percent raise. The managers could award only one more 6 percent raise and therefore decided to split a 3 percent and a 6 percent raise between the two engineers, awarding each a 4.5 percent raise.

their rankings. On the list the year I was present, the comments about all the top ten engineers mentioned the long hours they worked. Number one on the list was Max, and the comment following his name read: "Works 80–100 hours/week, top quality work." The second on the list was noted for working similarly long hours. Comments about others in the top ten included: "works days and nights" and "works 80 hours per week." In contrast, the comments about those at the bottom of the list all referred negatively to the level of commitment, as assessed by hours worked. The bottom three comments were "average contribution," "light work load," and "minimal contribution." Clearly, managers notice the hours that the engineers work and use these observations as a criterion in ranking them.

Price of Nonconformity

Success at work requires producing one's own visible, individual deliverables. It also requires being willing to accommodate the demands of the work, doing whatever is asked whenever one is asked to do it. Simply being present at work is also required to validate one's contribution and demonstrate one's commitment to the job. Engineers who want to succeed go to great lengths to do what is expected of them. Even when they recognize that what they are being asked to do will not achieve the desired goals, they make every attempt to comply because they perceive that this behavior is a requirement for success.

Some engineers, however, cannot or will not endure all the demands imposed on them. Jane, for example, gives family higher priority than work. She explained, "I work because I want to be intellectually stimulated during the day. . . . I want to have colleagues to talk to. . . . I would go crazy staying home all the time." She added, "I will give 100 percent while I am here but I have decided work is not my main goal in life. Work is a means to other ends. . . . I used to work those long hours. Then I just decided, this is not really how I want to spend my life. . . . I have just changed my personal goals. I have decided that kids will come before my career. Some people when they first arrive put in the hours; some of them continue; but others like me decide differently."

As a result, Jane is not regarded as a committed employee. At one point, the senior software manager went so far as to offer Jane's project team leader, Laura, a choice. According to Laura, "He asked me whether I wanted to keep Jane on the team, or whether I would prefer a different engineer who showed a greater commitment to the work." Laura decided to keep Jane as a member of her group. Jane's peers and managers, however, continued to show little respect for her.

Other individuals believe they must meet the demands at home but are less willing to concede their career advancement. They try to find alternative ways of working that make it possible to meet responsibilities both at work and outside of work. Chris, for example, had to leave work three days a week by four-thirty. His wife worked evenings, and she insisted that he be home to care for their son before she left. When he was behind schedule, Chris would work Saturdays instead of Mondays in order to increase his productivity. According to Chris, "Saturdays are at least twice as productive as Mondays . . . [because] there are no interruptions."

At one point during the project, Chris substituted several Saturdays for Mondays and met his next deadline ahead of schedule. Chris declared, "I feel like I deserve a pat on the back for my accomplishments." Instead, the same manager who had accepted his alternative work schedule became irritated because as the deadline approached the rest of the team was also working Saturdays; however, unlike Chris, they were not taking Mondays off to compensate. The manager saw the other team members as putting in the extra effort when it counted and faulted Chris, who had worked steadily throughout and did not need to put in this extra time. In the end, when his level of commitment was being judged, the fact that Chris was the only member of the group who was on schedule seemed to go unnoticed.

Kate, whose case I describe in detail in Chapter 9, also tried to create an alternative way of working which would permit her to limit her hours and still meet her work demands. She decided to work at home one day a week. Within a year she dropped in ranking from a "premium" to a "below-average" employee.[4] Those who put up modest resistance to work demands and find alternative ways to complete their deliverables do not lose their jobs, at least for now. They do, however, sacrifice reward and recognition at work. Moreover, they live in fear that they may be the next laid off.

Layoffs at Work

In December employees found out that Ditto was planning to lay off thousands of people over the next two years. The first round of layoffs would occur in January, but no one knew who or how many employees would be terminated. Most people believed that one's job was safer if one was working on a project that had funding; PEARL had received such funding in September.

From December through mid-January, including Christmas vacation, engineers waited for further news. Finally, on January 16 workers were laid off in the downtown office, signaling that layoffs would soon occur at the Ditto site I studied. Tuesday, January 17, was a bleak day in Building 113. As employees arrived, some received pink slips indicating immediate termination of their employment. The rest were expected to continue working as if nothing had happened. Needless to say, little work got done that day.

None of the members of the software group I studied and only four of the forty-five members of the product team were laid off, but the layoffs affected everyone's attitude. Engineers expressed anger toward the company and unwillingness to give so much to a company that would lay off fellow employees even when it was making a profit. At the same time, the engineers who kept their jobs spoke of "feeling lucky" and "being privileged." Most feared that they might be "the next to go" and believed that

---

[4] Of the seventeen engineers I studied, ten resisted the demands on their time at work. Seven of the ten had resigned themselves to the negative career implications associated with limiting the time they spent at work; the other three were more frustrated by the tradeoffs they had to make. They wanted to succeed at work and to meet the demands on their time outside of work. In Perlow forthcoming, I explore in detail the responses of both the engineers and their spouses to the temporal demands put on the engineers at work.

the precarious employment situation made it necessary to work particularly hard to protect their jobs.

If conforming to the criteria for success was important before the layoffs, the pressure for conformity now became intense. Engineers employed at Ditto for many years and content to remain at their current job level suddenly worried that their lack of advancement would prove problematic. Individuals who had never wanted to make work their first priority now felt pressure to give their all to the organization simply to retain their jobs. Engineers who had intended to remain at Ditto for the duration of their careers felt compelled to reassess their plans, fearing that they no longer might have that option.

One of the three project team leaders, Paul, for example, said he no longer had a desire to climb the career ladder. He would prefer to spend the extra hours on either end of the workday at home with his family. In the environment generated by the layoffs, however, he could not make this choice. He noted, "Layoffs are in the air, and just staying at my level is a very risky strategy. The next round of layoffs could hit any time, and I will be gone if I do not continue to aspire to new levels. They do not want guys like me getting old and standing still. They would prefer the young guys who are always eager to do more." Paul now felt compelled to put more time into his work than he would have liked. Even Max, who is a star and knows it, acknowledged that "the best engineers have to worry in this environment."

As a result of the pressure to put in the time and the fear of losing one's job, engineers all work hard. Nevertheless, they vary in how much time they put in and how willing they are to accommodate a last-minute crisis. Both the work demands and the variation in individual responses have profound effects on engineers' home lives. I had the unique opportunity to visit engineers' homes and interview their spouses. In the next chapter, I describe the tradeoffs engineers make between work and home life and the effects on both themselves and their spouses.

4

Home Life: Tradeoffs between Work and Family

"It was in the thirties. Ice and snow were everywhere. Trees and power lines were down. We had no electricity; we had no heat; we had nothing but a wood-burning stove. I was home alone with our nine-year-old daughter. For six days and six nights we hovered over the stove, desperately trying to keep warm." Allan's wife, Kim, was describing to me the ice storm of 1991. The city had been declared a national disaster area. Allan was scheduled to leave on a business trip to Japan, but the airport was closed, and the trip was postponed for a day. When the airport reopened, Allan left his wife and daughter to fend for themselves. On previous trips to Japan he had been chastised for billing calls home more than once a week. This time he didn't call home for six days. When he finally did call, his family still had no power. His wife and child were freezing, scared, and exhausted. Moreover, they were bitter that they had been deserted. Kim told me:

> Our neighbors were horrified. They couldn't believe that Allan would leave me. I was the most hurt and angry of anyone, but I was busy defending him. Allan was in a lose, lose situation. He was afraid of shirking on his work responsibilities, but totally abandoning his wife in a city that had been declared a national disaster was shirking on his family responsibilities. . . .

Once he called and found out the situation he did come home
the next day.

Allan described his decision to come home:

> I felt I had done enough in Japan. I had been to all the meetings,
> and I had done the best job I could do. I felt my team could han-
> dle the rest without me. My wife needed me more, and so I
> left. . . . I left without having the opportunity to ask my boss. I
> just decided I needed to go, and I left. . . . I was trying to meet
> my commitments to everyone, but in the process I managed to
> piss everyone off. My manager is still mad at me. My wife is still
> mad at me.

Allan loved his wife and daughter. Yet, he was caught up in the demands of his work, and he often failed to notice how his preoccu-
pation with the job burdened his family. At this point, his wife
rarely put up a fight, but she harbored great resentment toward
Allan and toward Ditto. "Families are locked out from the start,"
Kim noted. "The security system doesn't let anyone in the door,
and you are locked out from there on. You are locked out of trips,
recreational activities, dinners and celebrations. . . . Families are
not a part of the place!"

Kim, herself a social worker, worked three days a week at the
university hospital. She explained: "Allan used to be responsible to
empty the dishwasher in the morning before he went to work.
Now even that is more than he can handle. I used to try to force
him to help around the house, but it would always result in an ar-
gument. Now, I don't even try. I fear that he is so stressed by work
that he will not be able to handle anything else." And then she
added only half jokingly, "I would rather have a husband than a
dead husband." She said, "I have decided it is just easier to
do things myself rather than getting angry. I am too scared about
his health to have a fight." According to Kim, "Allan is experiencing all sorts of physical stress from work that is manifesting
in side effects. I want to call the doctor, but he refuses. . . . I am
so angry at the company that I would not want them at the fu-
neral. I feel so strongly that I actually think these thoughts, and
that scares me. I just think that after his death, then they would all

act so sympathetic, and yet, no one is doing anything about it now."

While Kim said she had stopped putting pressure on Allan to help around the house because she feared she "could be the one to put him over the edge," she could go on for hours telling stories about events Allan had missed, responsibilities he had shirked, and things she would have liked but could never have asked him to do. One Saturday, for example, she was feeling sick and was depressed about a close relative who had recently died. She said:

> It was a rough morning. I wasn't feeling well and then Rachel [their daughter] broke a lamp. I tried several times during the day to call Allan and tell him to come home. I needed help. I expected him home for lunch. I kept calling, but there was no answer. . . . I was so angry that around four o'clock I took my daughter and marched off to the jeweler and bought a very expensive diamond and pearl ring, in an attempt to console myself. . . . When I got home there was no sign of Allan, but I was feeling better, and I figured he would be home soon. I cooked dinner. . . . But, he never did come home for dinner. . . . He never called, and he didn't get home until nine-thirty that night. I was angry and I let him know that. . . . I threatened him that if he didn't come home it would cost him thousands of dollars because I would buy other things as well. . . . He had gotten wrapped up in working on something in the lab and just lost track of time. . . . He has never done anything quite like it again. . . . He still loses track of time, but he tries to be better about calling.

The only responsibility Allan still had was taking their daughter to piano lessons. Kim believed Allan liked to take her, to stay with her, and to sit with her while she practiced. Still, Kim said, "As much as he wants to do this with Rachel, he is never on time. He will come running into the house at 5:55 to get her for her six o'clock piano lesson, if he comes home at all." Recently, for example,

> He picked her up at six o'clock and took her. But then he left a note on the kitchen counter saying that he had to return to work, and could I please pick her up. . . . I happened to stay late at work that night, thinking that Rachel was with her father and

so there was no reason for me to hurry home. . . . When I walked in the door at seven-thirty the phone was ringing. It was Rachel. I rushed out to get her. . . . I was very angry that Allan would just abandon her and not make any attempt to get hold of me. He certainly should have made more effort than just to leave a message where I might never get it. . . . It is the only responsibility he has left, and I cannot even count on him for that.

I was still at Allan and Kim's house at 5:15 P.M. when the phone rang. It was Rachel. She wanted to be picked up. I heard Kim say into the receiver, "Dad will pick you up at five-thirty." But Rachel yelled back, so loud that I could hear her through the phone, "Mom please don't leave me here. You know Dad will never come. Mom please don't leave me here. I am the last one here. Please don't leave me here another time. Please Mom. Please." Kim finally agreed to pick her up. She put down the receiver and turned to me and said, "You see what I mean. We just don't trust him. He has let us down too many times."

Allan was late for everything, Kim said. "He shows up in the third period of school open houses and at the end of basketball games, if he makes it at all. He missed both my MSW graduation and when Rachel won the fourth grade role model contest." She offered, "It is always something: a vendor is visiting, a presentation to the vice-president, or losing track of time. . . . There always seems to be something important, some reason why he cannot be home."

Kim believed the recent layoffs had only added another component to Allan's stress. "After all," she noted, "his income does support the family." She explained: "My theory is that Ditto is trying to keep up with the Japanese and the Japanese work very long hours. Allan tells me stories about his trips to Japan. I know they work until midnight. I also read the booklets on Japan. I know they have no time for their families. They have a wife who takes care of everything and they have very traditional views about women." She added, "I recently read about a Japanese wonder drug 'Regain.' It is filled with caffeine and nicotine and enables you to work harder and longer."

Kim held out little hope for change. She seemed desperate for any suggestions about how to improve her life and Allan's. She admitted, "Divorce may be my only answer. For Allan, I just don't know. I wish Ditto cared more about the mental health of its people. . . . The facade that they are all so fortunate to have a job is absurd."

Female Spouses

Kim's experience at home highlights one extreme case. Her husband had a desire to succeed, and she suffered because he was often stressed, unavailable, unaware, and unhelpful at home. Other spouses have similar experiences. Pat, the wife of the software manager, Zeth, echoed Kim's discontent. Like Kim, she worked three days a week in a service-related field. She said: "I once gave him [Zeth] a two-page list of what he might do around the house and asked him to circle those tasks he would be responsible for. All he circled was taking out the trash. You better believe if all he is going to do is take out the trash, then I am never going to do it, even if it piles up all over. . . . I wait until he does it."

Of the seventeen software engineers, twelve were married (see Table 1). Only two of the engineers declined my request to interview their spouses. Both were men married to women who did not work outside the home. It is likely that they declined because they knew how unhappy their wives were. Matt, whose story is told in Chapter 5, reported: "I do not know what she will tell you. I know that she is very displeased with me and does not understand the hours that I am working. . . . I am afraid of what she might say." My assumption that Matt refused to let me interview his wife because of her dissatisfaction with their home life was reinforced when he reported the following exchange one Monday morning: "This weekend, a guy from down the hall approached me and said, 'You are always here. Is your wife unhappy with you, too?' I was relieved to find out that I was not the only one who is always in trouble for being at work."

Unlike Kim and Pat and, I believe, the two spouses I never met, Heather insisted that her husband, Chris, be home at night and do his share of the household chores and child care. "If he

TABLE 1

Family characteristics

	Number of children	Employment of spouse outside the home
Female engineer (spouse)		
Laura (Rick)	3	full-time
Kate (Pete)	3	full-time
Sarah (Tom)	1	full-time
Jane (Dan)	1	full-time
Male engineer (spouse)		
Stan (Lisa)	0	full-time
Zeth (Pat)	3	part-time
Paul (Beth)	4	part-time
Allan (Kim)	1	part-time
Chris (Heather)	1	part-time
John (Natalie)	1	part-time
Matt (n.a.)	2	none
Jerry (n.a.)	4	none
Max (single)	—	—
Andy (single)	—	—
Ben (single)	—	—
George (single)	—	—
Frank (single)	—	—

isn't paid for overtime," she said, "he should not work it." As Chris's manager said, "Chris's wife doesn't let him off the hook easily. He has strict hard stops everyday." Although husband and wife agreed that Heather's job was secondary, this assessment did not translate into Chris's work ruling their lives. On the contrary, Heather established constraints on what she was willing to accept in terms of Chris's work demands. In the odd crisis, Chris accommodated work, but he did not regularly make the accommodations associated with promotions, raises and big bonuses at Ditto. While Chris struggled with the tradeoffs he had to make at work more than any of the other male engineers whose spouses I have described so far, his wife was the most content.

Family situations like Chris and Heather's turned out repeatedly to generate the same response. When a male engineer made sacrifices at work for home, his spouse expressed satisfaction while he expressed conflicts between a desire to spend time at home and a desire to succeed at work. In contrast, male engineers who did not make these sacrifices at work, expressed less turmoil and did not perceive their devotion of time to work as problematic for themselves or their families. Their wives, however, were dissatisfied with what they perceived as an inequitable division of family responsibilities.

All of the spouses I have described so far are women; all worked at most part-time. In my sample of twelve married couples, seven of the eight married male engineers had children, and all seven were married to women who worked at most part-time. The eighth couple had not yet had children and both spouses worked full-time.

Some of the female spouses received more help from their husbands than others, either because, like Heather, they made explicit demands or because their husbands chose on their own to make family a priority. Regardless of how much help these women received or why they received it, however, all of them intentionally chose not to work full-time so that they could spend the hours at home that they felt were required to maintain the house and family. None of these women counted on their husbands to share equally at home.

Male Spouses

In contrast to the eight female spouses, of whom all who had children worked at most part-time, the four male spouses all had children and all worked full-time. Each of these four couples employed some sort of day care provider for their children. The remainder of the child care and household chores became a "second shift" (Hochschild, 1989) added to their two full-time careers.

Among these four male spouses, three worked at Ditto, two in positions lower than their wives' and one at the level of his wife's manager. The fourth male spouse taught middle school. All four of these men contributed at home. None, however, except possibly Tom, contributed more than his wife.

While Sarah worked, Tom, picked up their daughter from the baby-sitter, brought her home, made dinner, fed her, bathed her, played with her, and put her to bed. He appeared to be a committed, caring father. He admitted: "It gets hard having to be a single parent every night of the week. I love Stephanie and spending time with her, but sometimes it just gets to be too much. . . . I don't really understand what Sarah is doing, but I always give her the benefit of the doubt. Still sometimes I just think to myself, damn, this is getting old."

Pete, though he did less than Tom, also shared much of the responsibility at home while his wife, Kate, worked. According to Pete: "I pick the kids up from day care and bring them home. I spend time with them until Kate gets home, but bedtime is Kate's responsibility. I can do the things I do for the kids, but I am not their mother. These things should be a mother's responsibility. When she is not around I do them out of necessity." Pete, however, like Heather, set limits. He was unwilling to be left with more to do at home than he felt was his share. He said: "After 7:30 I am too tired to deal with the kids. I find being with them very stressful. . . . Kate makes sure to be home on time every night. . . . Otherwise we have a fight." Kate got the children up, dressed, and ready for school. She also did all the evening chores.

Unlike either Tom or Pete, Dan expressed little resentment about his wife Jane's work. According to Dan, "I don't know if Jane's work is stressful, demanding, or challenging. It seems that she manages fine and there seem to be no negative side effects on her or our relationship." The major difference was Jane's priorities. As mentioned in the last chapter, for Jane, family came first; there was no conflict. She would not let her work infringe on her personal life. As a result, her home life was the most satisfying for her spouse of the four dual-career couples, but her career also suffered most.

The other two female engineers I've mentioned, Kate and Sarah, put in more time at work than Jane, and their husbands were more frustrated with the division of labor at home. Laura and Rick were different. Laura put in even more time at work than either Kate or Sarah; yet Rick was less, not more, resentful than either Tom or Pete about the division of labor at home. The difference is the role that Rick was expected to play. As described in Chapter 2, Laura bore most of the responsibility for child care and household chores on top of her intense determination to succeed at work. Rick shared Laura's burning desire to succeed but not her concerns about their children's care. Rick was more distressed about the lack of time he had to do things in life he enjoys. He noted, "Time is a precious commodity. I will pay for things that save time. . . . My work may suffer slightly. But more than that, I don't have the personal time to do the things I like in life. I don't have time to do things I like—like playing golf." Laura had a very different experience of the demands that result when two individuals try to manage two successful careers and a family. She found she did not have enough time for either her work or her family, let alone herself. The stress she endured is indicative of how problematic it is to balance a successful career and primary responsibility at home.[1]

Among the four dual-career couples with children, the level of satisfaction of the male spouse with his home life did not directly relate to the time his wife devoted to her career. The two husbands who expressed the most satisfaction, Dan and Rick, were married to women who represented opposite ends of the spectrum in terms of commitment to work: Jane put her family first, while Laura was unwilling to sacrifice work for family. The similarity, however, is that Jane and Laura did not expect their husbands to contribute as much at home as either Kate or Sarah did. Jane sacrificed her career to find time for her family. Laura sacrificed her own personal well-being.

In the end, none of the four dual-career couples managed to balance two successful careers and a home life to their own satisfaction. All found that at least something had to go. There simply was

[1] That Laura is the only woman in my sample who tries to manage so many demands on her time is not indicative of how common this scenario is among ambitious professional women; it does, however, indicate the difficulty individuals face when trying to balance both a career and family and the reason so many employees search for alternatives. See, for example, Deborah Swiss and Judith Walker's (1993) description of how female graduates of Harvard's medical, business, and law schools struggle to balance their careers and their family lives.

not enough time. Laura and Rick appeared to come the closest, but Laura was always exhausted and she worried that her children suffered from lack of parental attention. She also worried that she was not putting enough time into her work. Rick was apparently oblivious to most of Laura's struggles and to the possibility that their children were experiencing parental neglect.

High Costs at Home

At Ditto success depends on demonstrating commitment to one's career, but the more time engineers invest in their work, the more difficult it is for them to contribute at home. Some of the engineers will not make the tradeoffs at home necessary for success at work. Their spouses tend to be most satisfied with their family life, but most of these engineers live in fear of the consequences at work. Some also feel deprived of an important aspect of their lives, namely, the opportunity to be successful at work. In contrast, many of the most successful engineers let their careers dominate their lives. Matt compared his work environment to a battle he must fight. He said, "Right now at work, I need to be single-minded. I must make whatever sacrifices are necessary. . . . The challenges we are facing are immense. It is like a war—a battle—you have to sacrifice a lot of things in order to achieve the objective." Matt further noted, "I am a go-getter and you cannot stop me when I want to get something. . . . When I am in this mindset I don't allow anything to disturb me. Only when it is done, will I sit back and relax. But until then, I must keep my mind focused."

The chance that Matt will ever "sit back and relax" for long is slim. The reward for hard work is a new position that demands even more hard work, more stress, and more sacrifices in one's life outside of work. Tracy Kidder (1981) captures this phenomenon well:

> They didn't have to name the bigger game. Everyone who had been on the team for a while knew what it was called. It didn't involve stock options. . . . The bigger game was "pinball." . . . "You win one game, you get to play another. You win with this machine, you get to build the next." Pinball was what counted.

It was the tacit promise that lay behind signing up, at least for some. . . . "I said, 'I will do this, I want to do it. I recognize from the beginning it's gonna be a tough job. I'll have to work hard, and if we do a good job, we get to do it again.' " (P. 228)

Individuals who "play pinball" are rewarded, but there are consequences too and often the players do not recognize the high costs until it is too late. In *Breaking the Mold*, Lotte Bailyn provides a vivid description of the regret felt by one hardworking senior executive when she realized what she had missed.

If I had it to do all over again, I think I would do things very differently. . . . I think I probably would have taken off several years instead of choosing to go right back to work. . . . I'm not sure I'd have the guts to do it that way, but my relationship with my son to this day is mediocre to poor and I think it's traceable back to [the fact that] I had an escape valve. . . . No one's going to write on my tombstone "Nancy Wright, senior executive of [company]." . . . No one will remember, hopefully, when I die at eighty-five, that I even worked here. But hopefully my children, who I haven't done a real terrific job raising, will get through whatever resentment they feel about that and we will have been able to establish a relationship where they will care to write on my tombstone, "She was a loving mother." (Pp. 61–62)

It may not be possible to achieve both success at work and a good home life. Choosing one may require forgoing the chance of accomplishing the other. In our society, more respect is granted those who choose success at work. In Part II, I explore how time is actually used at work and whether long hours are indeed the only way for the organization to achieve its productivity goals. I examine the assumption that this way of working, however damaging to home life, benefits the corporation. Further, I raise the possibility that alternative ways of working might achieve the organization's goals without requiring so many sacrifices at home both for oneself and one's family.

PART II

How Work Really Gets Done

To understand how work gets done and whether change is possible, it is important to have a rough understanding of what it means to do software engineering at Ditto.[1] The software engineer is supposed to complete a set of "individual deliverables," functions or features that they must produce or, in the language of the engineers, "implement." To implement a function or feature is to write the code that makes that function or feature operable. Each deliverable, therefore, requires writing lines of code to make

---

[1] There has been a general transition over the past fifty years from programming to software production (Kraft 1979). During this time programming has been fragmented and routinized. Early programmers approached programming as a whole task. They started with a desired outcome and the same group of programmers (or even the same individual) carried out the upfront planning, program design, instruction sequence, instruction entry, debugging, and maintenance. Gradually, the field of programming subdivided into coding, programming, and system analysis, generating a hierarchy of software engineers involved in product development (Kraft 1979). The lowest level of engineers are coders; they generally have junior/community college level training. The more skilled programmers, who have typically been trained in traditional engineering colleges, work on complete programs rather than program fragments. Finally, system analysts, who typically possess degrees from elite science institutions, design whole systems, languages, or other large-scale software. The engineers I studied at Ditto fall into the middle level of this classification.

something happen; for example, one deliverable might prompt the user to enter his or her name at a specified time.[2]

Engineers have a set of individual deliverables to be implemented for each "release date." By these dates all the deliverables must be compiled on a disk to be provided to the test groups and to other designated groups on the product team. During the design phase, release dates occur about once a month. During the testing phase, the software team makes a release once a week. The goal of the design phase, which for the PEARL team lasted from September until January, is to develop software. The goal of the testing phase, which lasted from February through June, is to solve design problems.

Each engineer's objective throughout the process is to produce his or her own *individual* deliverables. Engineers make a clear distinction among three types of work: the technical component of their work, the interactions they perceive to be directly related to their technical work, and the interactions necessary to facilitate the larger product's development. The engineers consider the technical component of their work "real engineering," the essence of which is developing algorithms, implementing functions, and debugging code. Real engineering requires the application of scientific principles and independent creativity; it uses the skills the engineers acquired in school. As one engineer summed it up, "Real engineering is what I thought I was hired to do."[3]

---

[2] Because of the extreme time pressure to develop PEARL, much of the framework for the code was bought from external vendors, and this strategy deprived the engineers of the degree of control to which they were accustomed. They viewed their work as adding code to a skeleton, and many complained that the work did not demand the originality and creativity they find stimulating. As one manager explained, however, "The engineers complain that their work is not challenging, but it is the work of the future. . . . They need to redefine what it means to do challenging work." He offered an example, "How many times do you think a mechanical engineer has designed a screw lately? They don't! They integrate them into their projects."

[3] Robert Zussman (1985) notes that engineers have both engineering and administrative responsibilities. Stephen Crawford (1989) found that the work performed by engineers includes technical conceptualization, technical execution, meetings, contracts with departments, technical writing, administration, relations with subordinates, relations with colleagues, and relations with supervisors. Crawford studied two organizations. In one, engineers spent 55 percent of their time, and, in the other, 35 percent, on work categorized as technical conceptualization and technical execution—what engineers consider "real engineering." The rest of the time was spent on activities not classified by engineers as "real engineering." In Perlow 1994 I detail the hierarchy of engineering activities.

Nothing else, whether it involves integrating, helping, checking, or planning, is considered real engineering. Instead, interactive activities are perceived as interruptions to one's real work.[4] As one engineer commented, "The biggest frustration of my job is always having to help others and not getting my own work done." Another engineer complained, "Now that I manage four people, this leaves me without a job. I spend my time telling them what to do, statusing things, and going to meetings."

Part II consists of three chapters that explore the role of interactive activities in the engineering work process. In Chapter 5, I present two narratives that illustrate variations in how individuals give and receive help and elaborate on the effects of these different ways of helping on getting the work done. In Chapter 6, I describe more generally the typical ways of interacting among the engineers, showing that interactions are critical, but that their timing is problematic. In Chapter 7, I describe the crisis mentality that drives engineers to treat the completion of their individual deliverables and the associated interactions as urgent and results in constant interruptions. Part II concludes in Chapter 8 with a description of the "vicious work time cycle" that results from the current reward system, disruptive way of interacting, and crisis mentality.

---

[4] John Van Maanen and Stephen Barley (1984) discuss the conflict that exists between occupational roles and organizational demands. The expressed preference for real engineering over interactive work is an example of what they call "occupational-organizational tension." Lotte Bailyn and I have suggested (Perlow and Bailyn 1997) that not all engineers prefer real engineering. Some express a preference for real engineering only because the culture of engineering promotes real engineering above all else. Engineers who might actually prefer interactive work repress their desires, despite the importance of interaction for product development. Both the engineers who prefer interactive work and the organization that requires it lose out. Judith S. McIlwee and J. Gregg Robinson's (1992) finding that this preference for interactive work is particularly strong among female engineers implies that women may be more adversely affected than men by the dominant culture of engineering.

5

Help and Helping: Matt's and Sarah's Stories

Sarah embodies the approach toward helping most common among the software engineers. She is under much pressure and feels she cannot waste time if she needs help. She feels no compunction about interrupting others whenever she needs help. She, however, is not very responsive to others' requests for help. She feels she has no time to help them.

Matt exemplifies an opposite and much less common approach. He is always willing to help others and is very concerned about how he affects others' work time. Moreover, Matt possessed a unique knowledge base that no one else on the software team had. He was the only team member with prior experience developing a printer. His knowledge combined with his natural tendency to respond to others' needs without asking for much in return made him a tremendous resource for the team. Given the amount of time he spent helping others, however, he found it difficult to complete his own work on time.

A Day in the Life of Sarah

On a Thursday in early December, I asked Sarah to keep track of a randomly chosen day.[1] The November 22 release had finally been

---

[1]One should keep in mind that Sarah's husband, Tom, was the male spouse who took on the most responsibility at home of the male spouses I studied.

delivered a few days late, and now all attention was focused on the December 20 release, just over a week away. She reported the following:

6:00	The baby woke up crying.
6:00–6:30	I fed the baby.
6:30–8:15	My husband played with the baby. I went back to sleep.
8:15	My husband woke me up. He left for work.
8:15–9:00	I got myself and the baby ready.
9:15	Arrived at the baby-sitter's. The baby was screaming, and the baby-sitter was busy.
9:15–9:30	I stayed to feed the baby.
9:30–10:00	Drove to work.
10:00	Arrived at work.
10:00–11:00	I initiated a conversation with Laura. (Yesterday I had come across a big design flaw, and I was very concerned about it. There is a requirements problem.) We decided we needed to meet with Pat in the afternoon. We set up a meeting for three o'clock.
11:00–12:00	I initiated a conversation with Chip. I needed some background information. He was available, so I bugged him. (I am a very interruptive person. I have no time to waste, so I look for expertise.)
12:00–12:30	I prepared slides for the three o'clock meeting.
12:30–12:45	I asked Matt a couple of quick questions.
12:45–1:00	I finished my slides.
1:00–2:30	We had a team meeting to discuss our priorities. (We are behind schedule, but the group is pretending we will make it. There is a big sense of denial going on. I voiced the problem. Laura got angry and accused me of being flip. She won't admit that there is a big problem brewing.)
2:30–3:00	The team sat around and bull shitted.
3:00–4:30	Laura and I met with Pat. I presented the problem and proposed my solution. I got their confirmation.

4:30–5:00	I stopped by to see Roy. He answered my question about supervisor rights. Then we chatted about sports.
5:00	I left for school.
6:30–9:30	Attended class.
10:30	Arrived home. My husband was already asleep.
10:30–1:00	I watched TV and vegetated.
1:00	I went to bed.

About her own work style Sarah said: "I'm one of those kinds of people that will ask anybody. I do not care if they work in our group, if they want to help me, or if they do not want to help me. If I need to get something done, I'll find somebody to help me; that is just the way I am. If I need to get something done, I'll just start putting the feelers out, looking for help. If I do not know it, there is no sense in sitting there wasting my time. I just go look for expertise." Sarah recognized that this might not be the most effective way to work, but she blamed it on the schedule. "I have no time to waste trying to figure something out that I do not understand." She did admit, "If I did it myself, I might learn more, such that next time I would be better prepared . . . but that type of long-term investment is impossible given the schedule."

A Day in the Life of Matt

As with Sarah, I asked Matt to keep track of a randomly chosen day, a Wednesday a few days before the November 22 release.[2] He reported the following:

6:00	Woke up.
6:00–6:40	Showered. Got dressed. Ate breakfast.
6:40	Left home.
7:00	Went to bank to get money.
7:10	Arrived at work.

---

[2]One should keep in mind that Matt was one of the two engineers who would not let me interview his wife.

7:10–8:50	I worked uninterrupted on my computer.
8:50–9:00	Sam and Mike stopped by to discuss a question about the server. (I had already told them they had an account. This was an unnecessary interruption. They could have figured it out themselves.)
9:00–9:23	Worked uninterrupted.
9:23–9:28	Roy called me to the front. He had forgotten his badge and needed to be signed into the building.
9:28	I returned to work.
9:30–9:54	Chris and Jane were debugging and hit a problem. They asked for suggestions.
9:54–10:06	While I was helping them, Sam and Mike came back with more questions.
10:06–10:10	Jane came by for some information on technical support. I gave her the form and told her how to fill it out.
10:10–10:30	Chris was having trouble with the printer in the lab. He had not yet met Jake, the new technical assistant. I introduced them.
10:30–12:00	I developed software.
12:00–12:15	I read a technical article that I thought might help me figure out the code.
12:15–1:00	I took a break and ate lunch at my desk.
1:00–1:45	I went back to developing software.
1:45–1:50	Sarah had a question about setting up the programming environment. I helped her.
1:50–2:00	I went back to developing software.
2:00–2:10	Sarah came back with another question.
2:10–2:40	I went to see Sam. I wanted to know how things were working out. He told me something was not right. I helped him. We had a general discussion about networks.
2:40–2:45	I returned to work.
2:45–2:50	Max came by. He needed some advice on something that was not working. I offered him a few suggestions.
2:50	I took a break to get some tea.
2:53–4:15	I returned to work.

4:15–4:20	Sarah had a configuration question.
4:20–5:00	I returned to work.
5:00–5:10	Tea time.
5:10–5:15	Sarah stopped by with more of the same.
5:15–5:20	I went to the lab to see how Max and Andy were doing.
5:20–8:00	I worked uninterrupted with my door closed.
8:00	I was getting ready to leave. My wife was waiting out front. I opened my office door and went to check something in the lab. I ran into Sarah. She was surprised to see that I was there even though my door had been closed. She asked for help. I helped her.
8:22	I left.
8:55–9:30	My wife and I arrived home. Dinner was ready. My wife had already eaten. I ate.
9:30–10:30	I paid some bills.
10:30	I went to bed.

Matt considered this day typical, both in terms of the number of times he was asked for help and in how late he stayed to get his own work done. He told me: "Last night, I called my wife at 6 P.M. and told her not to pick me up until 7 P.M., but at 7 P.M. I changed my mind again and called to ask for 8 P.M. We were supposed to meet outside the guard booth. . . . Around five minutes to eight, I started to pack up my stuff. I wanted to check one thing in the lab before I left. When I got to the lab, Sarah was there. She was having problems with her code. . . . I spent the next half an hour trying to help her understand her work so that she could continue without me." He added, "If she needs help, my first priority is to help her," but "when the conversation began to move away from helping her to a more social conversation, then I looked at my watch and said, 'Oops, I better go, my wife is waiting for me.'"

When I asked Matt why he had waited so long to tell Sarah that his wife was waiting, he replied: "It was my first priority to make sure she could do her work. She needed my help, and I didn't want her to feel uncomfortable asking questions. If I told her my wife was waiting, she would have stopped, and I did not want that. Once somebody starts the process flowing you do not want to discourage them. . . . My wife can wait. . . . People have what they call "hard stops," but I think you should be more flexible. If you go out there and have a flat tire, you still have thirty minutes you waste trying to change the tire. So you cannot really be hard about that. Why be hard when people need help?"

Matt reported that he was very willing to help others, but he expected people to learn in the process and then to be prepared themselves to share their newly acquired knowledge with others. "I want to facilitate the learning process. I want them to learn to do it by themselves. When I help, I try to just do enough to enable them to learn to do it on their own. I push them away to make them try. . . . I welcome them back if they need more direction." However, "I don't like people to send others to see me. I would rather that once I have helped them, that they in turn try to help the others themselves."

Giving Help

Matt promoted a system of learning and helping. Unlike Max, who responded to a question by taking over the problem, Matt consciously attempted to develop people's capacity to address the question themselves. He said, "It takes longer in the short term, but it pays off in the end."

Matt also recognized that others need support in order to work effectively. One day an engineer was very excited because she had just figured out the solution to the problem that had been impeding her progress. She went to Chris to show him, but he told her he was too busy and could not be bothered to take a look. She felt rejected. Matt explained:

> Sometimes you just need a pat on the back; you just need a
> boost. I do not think that Chris meant anything bad when he
> · said he was busy and did not want to check out her stuff. He
> probably was tied up in what he was doing. That is one thing
> about somebody like Chris, they can say no and then sit and do

what they were doing without feeling bad. This way Chris can make optimal use of his time. I just cannot do this. I know that she needed someone to go over and take an interest.

Because Matt had a reputation as a willing, supportive helper, he invited interruptions. Whenever there was a problem in the lab, Matt was the first software engineer the test group looked for, not because it was necessarily his problem but because they knew that when they turned to him for help he would be receptive. As a result, Matt spent much time working on other people's problems.

One day when I was shadowing Matt, one of the printers crashed in the testing lab. Someone from the testing group came to find Matt and tell him that a printer was down. This type of problem is considered an emergency because it brings all testing of that printer to a halt until the problem is fixed. At first, no one knows which software engineer is responsible for the piece of code that causes the specific problem. At least one engineer has to be generous enough with his or her time to conduct the initial investigation to identify the source of the problem. Matt was considered a likely candidate for this up-front problem identification not because he was better equipped to analyze problems but because he was responsive to these requests.

In this particular case, Matt went to examine the printer. He first thought the problem might be caused by the cable, and he went to get a new one, but the problem persisted. Then he decided that the type of computer might be at fault; so he went to a different lab to fetch a computer. He put it on a cart and wheeled it into the testing lab, but it didn't solve the problem either. At this point, Matt was not sure what was wrong, but he was fairly certain to whom the problem belonged. Just making this determination, however, had required him to spend over an hour on a problem that was not his.

Matt recounted a similar event the next day, but one that generated a different outcome. This time when someone came to ask for help, Matt reported:

> I was so busy that I had no choice but to say I couldn't deal with
> their problem this afternoon. By the time I was able to respond

the next morning, it was too late, the problem had been solved. . . . If I had been available I would have ended up wasting all of yesterday afternoon on something that turned out not to be my problem. . . . This is a classic example of how I end up wasting time on things that have nothing to do with me. . . . But, someone has to investigate them, and that often ends up being me. Up front, we just don't know whose problem it is.

Matt's generosity, clearly useful to those seeking help, attracted a disproportionate share of people's problems. Matt summed it up: "The problem with my work style is that responsiveness breeds more need for responsiveness, and I am so busy responding, I cannot get my own work done. Once I open myself up to doing something, I just cannot say no."

Sarah provided a stark contrast. She said, "If they [members of the testing group] have a problem, they should write it down and tell me about it at a mutually convenient time." She explained, "I am careful not to establish a reputation for being helpful because the test group will come to me all the time. I want them to think twice before they approach me."

Sarah suggested that she did not have time to take part in team-focused activities. She often skipped the "Sunset" meeting, where the software problems that came up in the test labs during the day were reviewed and assigned to the appropriate engineers. The more software engineers present at this meeting, the better able the group is to achieve a collective understanding of the problems and the more likely they are to assign each problem to the appropriate engineer. Yet, Sarah did not believe she needed to be at these meetings. Apparently, she did not feel compelled to share the responsibility of figuring out whose problems are whose, nor did she worry about being assigned problems that were not hers. She said if a problem was incorrectly assigned to her, "I have no trouble throwing it back over the wall to whoever I think should deal with it." Her determination of who has responsibility may be wrong, however, further wasting others' time. Her input in assigning problems up front in the Sunset meeting would likely have saved time for the group, but Sarah felt she simply did not have time to participate.

Getting Help

While Matt was always willing to help and support others, he hesitated to ask for help. On one occasion, he lacked the training necessary to complete a specific aspect of his deliverables. He had a lot of work to do and not enough time to learn what he needed to know, and he was exhausted. Someone had to help. Matt learned that an acquaintance, John, on a different program in a different division of the company possessed the necessary skills. Matt, though, did not feel comfortable asking John to take time away from his own work because he knew John would get no recognition for providing help. Even after Matt's manager approved the exchange between Matt and John with John's manager, Matt was still reluctant to take up much of John's time. Matt explained: "I know what happens around here all too well. No matter what is said, John will not be recognized for helping me. For John, all that matters is his own work. Helping me will only take time away from his work." Matt therefore tried to minimize his imposition: "I saved up all my questions and only disrupted John on an infrequent basis, instead of approaching him for each question."

In contrast, when Sarah needed help, she went out and got it. She was comfortable asking for help from those whom she would likely never repay. Yet she was reluctant to help others who would not be able to repay her. Matt had the opposite attitude: he would help anyone but hesitated to ask for help from others.

No Organizational Recognition for Helping

Managers did not acknowledge that Matt made a contribution to the team by playing such helpful roles. Rather, Matt's managers viewed both his tendency to help others and his tendency not to impose on others' time as problematic. They discouraged these behaviors. At one point, Matt approached the software manager and told him he was having a problem answering all the demands for his help and completing his deliverables on time. According to

Matt, he was told, "Do your own work first, and then if you want to help others, that is your choice, but do it on your own time." Matt was dissatisfied with this answer. He told me: "I know I am supposed to put my deliverables first, at the expense of all else, but that is very difficult when so many people need help, and they get stuck if I do not take the time to share my knowledge."

Matt's inability to say no to others particularly frustrated his project team leader. She insisted:

> He needs to get his own deliverables done, and it is my responsibility to shelter him from additional requests. When others, especially Zeth, approach Matt, he will never say no. Nor does he make clear the implications of doing the additional work he is given. If he is to help others, by default, his own work will suffer. However, Matt never raises this issue. . . . I have begged him to insist that all requests come through me, because at least I can help to prioritize how he spends his time. . . . Matt needs to focus on his own work. Otherwise, our group will never succeed.

Matt's managers, further, found him difficult to manage, especially in a crisis, because he did not want to disturb others by seeking their help. At one point, his project team leader said, "Matt needs to get help. We do not have time for him to figure it out on his own. We need him to get it done as soon as possible." When a crunch hit, Matt's managers would monitor him closely to ensure "he stays focused and does not waste any time trying to figure things out on his own. He needs to get help immediately if there is a problem."

No one disputed the importance of Matt's technical knowledge. He contributed to successful product development in ways far beyond producing his own deliverables. Yet, despite their importance, those aspects of his work remained, for the most part, invisible and unrewarded. Matt's helpfulness was recognized, but only as an impediment to the completion of his own deliverables. His conscientiousness about others' time, too, was mentioned only as a disadvantage.

The difference between Matt and an organizationally acknowledged superstar like Max is not technical competency or hours worked but allocation of time at work. Matt spent as many hours at work as Max did, but far more time helping others. In the end, Matt completed his deliverables but lacked time to exceed the expectations of his managers.[3]

Sarah, too, completed her deliverables, but her managers and peers perceived them as less technically demanding than Matt's. In addition, she worked fewer hours than Matt.[4] Yet, the major difference between Sarah and Matt is not their output or the hours they work but their work styles. This difference was never mentioned. Whenever Sarah perceived a problem as critical, she disrupted everyone and generated a ripple of crises. Work pressure did not affect Matt in the same way. He completed his work by maintaining a constant, intense pace over long periods of time. His work style was less overtly disruptive for the organization than Sarah's style. Yet Matt created his own set of problems for the group, since his deliverables had to be done if the product was to be completed.

Most engineers feel that they have little or no time to help others and behave more like Sarah than Matt. As a result, engineers are constantly interrupting each other and then complaining that they have no time to work uninterrupted and, therefore, that they cannot complete their real engineering on time. In the next chapter I explore in more detail how time is allocated between interactive work and "real engineering."

---

[3] Last year Matt received a 4.5 percent raise compared to Max's 6 percent raise. I estimate Matt's income to be slightly less than Max's—probably in the high $40,000s. Matt received no financial bonuses for outstanding performance. His raise did exceed the company average of 3 percent, but the reason apparently was his technical capabilities and his willingness to work long hours, not the help he provided his teammates.

[4] Sarah received a 3 percent raise. She was one grade level lower than both Max and Matt and probably earned an income in the mid $40,000s.

6

Constant Interruptions: Misuses of Time

To find out how much time engineers actually spend doing "real engineering"—individual technical problem solving—and how much time they spend interacting, I analyzed thirty-five daily logs kept by the twelve software engineers.[1] I considered the amount of time engineers spend alone and with others, but also what roles both individual and interactive time play in facilitating the completion of their individual deliverables and the work of the groups to which they belong.[2] For example, one Wednesday just after the November 22 release, I asked Andy to keep a log. He reported:

6:30	Woke to radio. Hit snooze.
6:50–7:35	Got up, showered, ate breakfast, and left house.
8:00	Arrived at work.

---

[1] The thirty-five logs come from the three days of tracking done by each of the twelve engineers. One engineer did not join the PEARL software group until after the first round of tracking data had been collected; hence, there are data for thirty-five rather than thirty-six days. For details, see the Methodological Appendix.

[2] The description of individuals' ways of sequencing activities presented in this chapter provides a new way of examining the use of time at work, which falls in between two levels of analysis. The literature to date on the temporal organization of work focuses either at the level of patterns of interaction, as will be described in Chapter 7 (i.e., Roy 1960; Zerubaval 1979) or at the level of turn-taking within an interaction (Goffman 1967, 1983; Sacks, Schegloff, and Jefferson 1974; Schegloff 1992). In this chapter, I consider individuals' sequencing of actions and interactions and how individuals' sequences affect one another and the group. In Perlow 1996, I further detail this approach and its theoretical and practical implications.

8:00–8:10	Checked mail; got coffee.
8:10–8:20	Sat down to work.
8:20–8:30	Interrupted myself to inform Dan and Sam that they were working on the wrong code. This was not constructive for me but could potentially save them a lot of time. This could have been avoided if we had received the proper code several days ago.
8:30–8:50	Worked on the computer.
8:50–9:00	Interrupted by Ben to talk about NAFTA debate on TV last night. Zeth joined the discussion.
9:00–9:45	Attended Milton's communication meeting.
9:45–9:50	Social conversation as I returned to lab.
9:50–10:20	Got back to lab and was immediately interrupted by Sam. He needed to try to bring up the new ethernet card on the bobcat board. We got it running by 10:20. Sam left.
10:20–10:30	I continued to play around with this.
10:30–11:10	Allan interrupted us to update us on the release plan. He then asked each of us for status. This was of some value to him and virtually no value to me. These status updates should be less frequent.
11:10–11:30	I actually got to work debugging my code.
11:30–12:45	Lunch at my desk. Did some non-work-related paper work. No interruptions.
12:45–1:35	Returned to lab. Immediately interrupted by Sam about ethernet card. We mucked around with it for about forty-five minutes. In the end, we determined that one card is bad, the other was okay. This was pretty much a waste of my time, but Sam has no other working system to try it on.
1:35–2:00	Immediately upon Sam's leaving, Fred showed up with some test patterns he needed to print. I spent twenty-five minutes helping him. This gave him some information he needed but was a waste of time for me.
2:00–2:15	Worked with Max integrating some changes we both made to some files. This was necessary interaction.

2:15–2:35	I interrupted Pat to talk about some requirement issues. (This was useful for both of us.)
2:35–3:00	Did my work.
3:00–3:05	Brief interruption by Roy, who asked if we could meet to discuss color rendering issues. We set a time.
3:05–4:35	Sam showed up with a Macintosh to try the ethernet card again. This occupied the next hour and a half. We determined that ethertalk does not work. The ESS rarely boots with the ethernet card attached. (This was totally disruptive to what I had planned for the afternoon.)
4:35–4:40	I took a break to make my draft pick for Fantasy Football.
4:40–4:50	Mark returned a call I left him regarding the ethernet problem but he was no help.
4:50–8:15	No interruptions. Actually got some work done.
8:15	Ran into trouble with Ben's code, which Max compiled before he left for school. I decided to go home.
8:45	Arrived home. Made dinner. Watched TV.
10:00	Paid bills, balanced checkbook.
11:30	Went to bed.

Andy's log is analyzed in Table 2. In analyzing each tracking log, I calculated the total amount of time spent at work each day and broke it down into individual work, interactions, and personal affairs. During the day represented in Table 2, Andy spent twelve hours and fifteen minutes at work, of which 39 percent was devoted to individual work, 49 percent to interactions, and 12 percent to personal affairs. Andy spent less time alone that day than was typical of the software engineers I studied. On average, the software engineers spend 57 percent of their time on individual work, 38 percent interacting, and 5 percent on personal affairs. However, on average, the engineers' days involve similar amounts of fragmentation. As Andy's log showed, individual time does not occur in one consecutive block, or even a few large blocks, but in very short blocks sandwiched between interactions.

TABLE 2

Analysis of Andy's day

Duration	Total time	Type of activity[a]	Characteristics of work interactions	
			Helpful[b]	Urgent[c]
8:00–8:10	10	P	—	—
8:10–8:20	10	I	—	—
8:20–8:30	10	X	Y	Y
8:30–8:50	20	I	—	—
8:50–9:00	10	X	—	—
9:00–9:45	45	X	Y	N
9:45–9:50	5	X	—	—
9:50–10:20	30	X	Y	N
10:20–10:30	10	I	—	—
10:30–11:10	40	X	Y	N
11:10–11:30	20	I	—	—
11:30–12:45	75	P	—	—
12:45–1:35	50	X	Y	N
1:35–2:00	25	X	Y	N
2:00–2:15	15	X	Y	N
2:15–2:35	20	X	Y	N
2:35–3:00	25	I	—	—
3:00–3:05	5	X	Y	N
3:05–4:35	90	X	Y	N
4:35–4:40	5	X	—	—
4:40–4:50	10	X	N	N
4:50–8:15	205	I	—	—

[a] I = Individual Time; X = Interactive Time; P = Personal Time.

[b] Based on engineer's perception of whether work interaction is helpful to either oneself or someone else involved. Y = Yes; N = No. Note that this column only has data for blocks of time spent on nonsocial interactions at work.

[c] Based on engineer's perception of whether work interaction is urgent. Y = Yes; N = No. Note that this column only has data for blocks of time spent on nonsocial interactions at work.

Andy had only one block of individual time that lasted over an hour (4:50–8:15).[3] More generally, for the engineers I studied, 75 percent of the blocks of time spent on individual deliverables were one hour or less in length, and of those blocks of time, 60 percent were half an hour or less in length (see Figure 3).

It is not surprising that engineers complain bitterly about not having time during the normal workday to get their individual work done. Most engineers believe that they need long blocks of uninterrupted time to complete their real engineering (and therefore to succeed at work). Yet, on average, only 36 percent of engineers' time occurs in uninterrupted blocks over one hour long. Engineers' days are spent continually flipping back and forth from individual to interactive work.

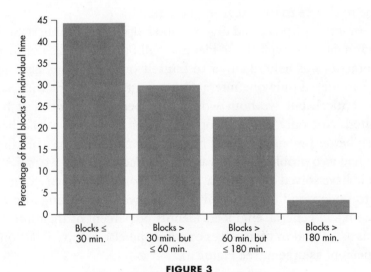

FIGURE 3
Distribution of blocks of individual time

[3] A block of time is defined as the number of consecutive minutes that an individual works either alone or with others. Interactions determine when a block of individual time begins and ends. It is noteworthy that Andy's one long block of individual time occurred after five o'clock. In general, I found no difference in lengths of blocks of individual time during the period from nine to five compared to the total workday. Because engineers often come in early and stay late in hope of avoiding interruptions, many engineers are present to interrupt each other, even during the hours at either end of the "normal" workday.

Moreover, engineers have little control over the fragmentation of their schedules. Most interactions (95 percent) occur spontaneously. Because engineers do not know when they will be interrupted, even long periods without interruption are not recognized as opportunities for deep concentration. Only in retrospect do the engineers realize that they have just had a long time to work alone. As one engineer said, "I am constantly looking over my shoulder, fearing that someone is about to throw something at me." This dread of interruptions is distracting and costs time. According to one engineer, "Working on Saturdays is much more productive. . . . I can sit down and work without always worrying that something is about to sidetrack me." Spontaneous interactions, thus, are distracting both because they fragment the workday and because they make it impossible for engineers to settle down with any confidence that they will have a significant block of time to devote to their real engineering.

In terms of perceived urgency and helpfulness of interactions, Andy's day was typical. He identified all but one of his nonsocial interactions as helpful either to himself or to someone else. Yet, he considered only one interaction urgent: "The work with Sam was critical, but we both would have been better off if it had waited. Not only was it inconvenient for me, but I would have been better prepared if I was further along in my own work first. We had two problems as it was. . . . If I had done my work first, I could have solved one of them. Then it would have been easier for us to understand the problem that Sam was introducing into the system." In general, engineers identify 96 percent of their interactions as helpful to themselves or someone else involved, but only 10 percent as urgent (see Figure 4).[4]

Types of Interactions

Despite the negative effects of interruptions, interactions are nonetheless critical to the work process. I have organized interac-

---

[4] In calculating the percentage of interactions that are helpful and urgent, I excluded socializing interactions, defining them as breaks from work, not work itself.

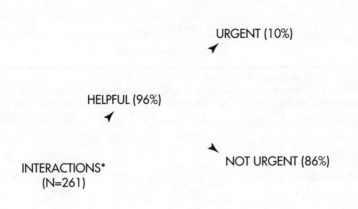

URGENT (10%)

HELPFUL (96%)

INTERACTIONS*
(N=261)

NOT URGENT (86%)

NOT HELPFUL (4%)

FIGURE 4
Helpfulness and urgency of interactions
*The interactions are from the 35 tracked days and include helping (129), checking (77), integrating (9), planning (12), and miscellaneous (34).

tions into six categories: helping, checking, integrating, planning, socializing, and miscellaneous (see Table 3).[5] Below, I describe the role that each of these types of interaction plays in the work process. Table 3 reports the frequency and duration of these types of interactions.

Helping is the most common type of interaction. When engineers confront barriers they often turn to other engineers for help. They ask either someone whose work will later be integrated with theirs or someone whose work is not connected with their own. The more directly related the work of the engineer asking for help

---

[5] I elaborate on only the visible interactions that are a recognized, although not rewarded, part of the process of software engineering. A colleague on my research team, Joyce Fletcher, studied engineers in the same product development division. She elaborates in great detail on the interactive activities that are not recognized as part of the engineer's job, identifying four main types of "invisible" interactions: those associated with preserving the life and well-being of the project; those related to empowering others to achieve and contribute to the project; those empowering oneself to achieve goals and contribute to the project; and those intended to create the social entity team. These "behind the scenes" interactions help to facilitate the visible interactions I document. For details, see Fletcher 1994.

TABLE 3

Types of interactions

Type of interaction[a]	Number of interactions observed (326)	Average length of interaction (in min)	% of total time at work (19,088 min)	Perceived as helpful (96%[b])	Perceived as urgent (10%[b])
Helping	129	20	14%	94%	9%
Checking	77	22	9%	98%	8%
Integrating	9	66	3%	100%	17%
Planning	12	32	2%	100%	25%
Socializing	65	29	10%	26%	0%
Miscellaneous	34	19	3%	96%	10%

[a]Over the course of 35 tracked days, 326 interactions were observed which lasted 7,821 minutes of the total 19,088 minutes engineers were at work.

[b]The overall percentage of both helpful and urgent interactions is higher because socializing interactions have been omitted. When socializing is included, the percentage of helpful interactions decreases from 96% to 80% and the percentage of urgent interactions decreases from 10% to 8%.

is to the helping engineer's work, the more likely that the engineer being asked for help will provide it in a timely fashion.[6]

Engineers also frequently inquire about one another's progress, and managers often check up on the engineers' work. The most common type of checking is a manager asking an engineer his or her "status" on a particular problem or issue. Managers check up on engineers both to provide resources and to allay their own fears that their engineers are in danger of failing to meet deadlines. Engineers check up on one another to gain a sense of where they are in relation to their peers. Much of this kind of information is exchanged in informal hallway conversations, whether between a manager and an engineer or between two engineers. Less frequently, the manager assembles the group and asks each engineer for a progress report.

---

[6] A useful distinction was noted by Andrea Campbell between "helping/teaching" and "helping/doing." Helping/teaching is designed to improve someone's ability to succeed. Helping/doing involves taking over for the other individual—completing another's task, gaining visibility, and reaping rewards at the other's expense.

At some points, engineers must work jointly to integrate their pieces of code. In such cases, the engineers involved share joint responsibility for putting the code together. Various degrees of integration occur throughout the project, ranging from brief, intermittent interactions for the purpose of assessing compatibility of code to continuous, sustained interactions during which several engineers sit together in front of a computer terminal to assemble code.

Occasionally, the engineers get together, with or without their manager, to plan how to proceed. The purpose of these gatherings is to coordinate the engineers' efforts and develop a strategy to proceed, allotting tasks to each individual.

Some interactions are not specifically work related. Although social interactions sometimes include conversations about work, their primary purpose is to provide a break. These interactions include hallway conversations, coffee breaks, and lunch.

Several types of interactive activities bring the software engineers into contact with individuals outside the software group. These interactions primarily include meetings with the larger project team and aiding members of the testing groups.[7] I classify these activities as miscellaneous because of the low frequency of each type.

---

[7] Software engineers attend a variety of meetings. At the Sunrise meeting every morning at eight-thirty members of the test lab provide feedback on the printer from the day before to all the project team leaders. Software engineers attend these meetings infrequently, either to stand in for their project team leader or to address a specific software problem on that day's agenda. In the testing phase of the product development cycle, there is also a Sunset meeting every afternoon at three, which focuses on the performance of the software from that day's tests. Although this meeting is not mandatory, most software engineers attend it.

Less frequently a communication meeting is held to provide the group updates. The product manager holds a communication meeting about once a week to discuss some topic with the product team. The division vice-president holds a communication meeting every few months to provide updates on the division.

Software engineers also have frequent interactions with members of the testing groups. There are two types of testing groups. One type comprises technicians who stress the printers in as many ways as possible, looking for problems such as incorrect messages to the user, failure of the printer to operate as planned, or worse, a crash of the printer. The employees in this test group act like "dumb" users, testing the printer for operability. The second type of test group is composed of system engineers, most of whom occupy grade levels higher than the software engineers themselves. These engineers test the software for applicability in a wide range of situations. The software engineers must provide support for problems that emerge from both test groups.

In addition to reporting the frequency and duration of types of interactions, Table 3 reports their perceived helpfulness and urgency. Almost all interactions are perceived as helping someone involved, but integrating and planning are more likely than checking to be perceived as urgent.

Engineers complain less about time spent integrating, planning, or even helping because they perceive these interactions as directly or indirectly facilitating completion of their own deliverables. In contrast, engineers distinctly dislike checking interactions. They complain that their managers constantly want updates. However helpful to the managers, engineers see checking as a waste of their own time. One irritated engineer asked rhetorically, "How am I supposed to make any progress when I spend so much time statusing my manager on what I have not yet accomplished?" Another engineer complained, "Everyone around here wastes so much time checking up on each other. Every morning our managers have a Sunrise meeting to update each other and resolve crises. They shift around our priorities. After the meeting, they come running to tell us what we should be working on. By the afternoon they come to shift everything again and we are back to doing what we were working on before the morning meeting." Managers themselves sometimes mock the purpose of checking interactions. One day the product manager, Milton, arranged an emergency meeting. He told me afterward, "This morning I called a meeting for 2 P.M. I know there was a reason. But when I got there, I couldn't even remember what the crisis was. So I just used the meeting to see how things were going."

Reflecting on the Problem

Engineers' biggest complaint about interactions is the amount of time they must spend on them. Contrary to engineers' perceptions, however, the problem seems to lie not with the time spent interacting but with the distraction that spontaneous interaction creates. Interactions are crucial to getting the job done. Code cannot be written without interaction among engineers, managers, and support staff. No one can successfully complete his or her own deliverables sitting alone in front of a computer. Rather, the work of software engineers requires both individual work and interaction (Bucciarelli 1988).

Whereas the vast majority of interactions (95 percent) occur spontaneously, however, almost all (86 percent) could be planned for a later time without negative repercussions (see Figure 4). Everyone involved therefore might benefit if these interactions were planned rather than spontaneous.[8] These findings highlight the importance of the timing of interactions.

Consider the implications for Henry Mintzberg's classic study of the daily activities of managers. The managers Mintzberg studied followed an interaction pattern characterized by "brevity, variety and fragmentation" (Mintzberg 1973, 31). Mintzberg describes a portion of a manager's day:

> A subordinate calls to report a fire in one of the facilities; then the mail, much of it insignificant, is processed; a subordinate interrupts to tell of an impending crisis with a public group; a retiring employee is ushered in to receive a plaque; later there is a discussion of bidding on a multi-million dollar contract; after that, the manager complains that office space in one department is being wasted. . . . Half of the observed activities were completed in less than nine minutes, and only one-tenth took more than an hour. (Pp. 31–33)

Mintzberg maintains that this pattern of interacting must be beneficial for these managers or else they would change it: "The five chief executives of my study appeared to be properly protected by their secretaries, and there was no reason to believe that these men were inferior delegators. In fact, there was evidence that they chose not to free themselves of interruption or to give themselves much

---

[8] My conclusion that "everyone involved might benefit" represents only the engineers' perspective on the urgency of their interactions. It could be that managers do not agree that interactions can wait. It is important to note, however, that only 19 percent of the interactions being discussed involve managers, and of those, 80 percent are checking interactions. Even managers comment on the absurdity of all the checking. Moreover, as I document in Chapter 10, after the managers agreed not to interrupt the engineers during blocks of quiet time, they came to recognize that even interactions they believed to be urgent, could wait. Of course some interactions are urgent, but the data indicate that the overwhelming majority, although treated as urgent, are not.

free time. To a large extent, it was the chief executives themselves who determined the durations of their activities" (p. 34).

Mintzberg may indeed be correct that managers choose this way of interacting and, moreover, that it is desirable for them. Neither Mintzberg, however, nor the managers he studied consider the effects of this interaction style on others in the organization. Managers like those Mintzberg studied are the people who often interrupt employees like the engineers I studied. If the effects of managers' interactions on those whom they manage are studied, one will likely find that they are at least partially negative. Such disruptions can impede attainment of the organization's goals. Clearly, this is not the intention of managers when they interact with their team members.

When evaluating the benefits of spontaneous interaction, one should not overlook the costs of interruption. According to George Mandler's (1982) "theory of interruptions," any event, external or internal to the individual, which prevents completion of some action, thought sequence, play, or processing structure triggers a person's autonomic nervous system, indicating to the person that immediate attention is required. The interruption is then brought into consciousness where repair and coping can take place. The arousal created in the process has been shown to have a variety of effects, mostly negative, on memory, attention, and efficiency of complex thought processes.[9]

While Mintzberg's work documents the critical role that interactions play in the work process, Mandler's theory highlights the importance of considering the disruptive effects of these interactions on the people involved. My research further suggests that the substantive effects of interactions are related to their timing. It may be that if an interaction is scheduled, the gains from interacting will accrue, but the drawbacks could be avoided. Currently, however, managers treat everything as urgent, and altering the

---

[9] Research has shown that arousal causes people to focus on central issues and away from peripheral ones; performance on central tasks therefore improves while performance on peripheral tasks declines (Weltman, Smith, and Egstrom 1971; Baddeley 1972). Arousal also has been shown to cause one to make earlier, overlearned, simpler responses (Barthol and Ku, 1959; Zajonc 1965). Furthermore, arousal has been found to reduce the number of cues a person processes, which improves performance if the person was previously processing irrelevant cues and hurts performance if a wide range of cues are needed to complete the task at hand (Easterbrook 1959; Watchel 1967).

timing of interactions seems infeasible to them. Crises perpetuate and so does the sense that all work is high priority and cannot be delayed. In the next chapter, I describe the crisis mentality and how it is perpetuated. In Part III, I explore the possibility for change.

7

Crisis Mentality: Rhythms of Work

Crises, not well-thought-out plans, dictate most days' work for the engineers.[1] As one engineer put it, "Around here we are always fighting fires. . . . We can never get our assigned work done, as planned." Another engineer complained, "I can hardly get my coat off before the crises start. Every morning my priorities seem to shift."

The problem as the engineers see it, is that everything is left until the last minute. As one software engineer explained: "Zeth [the software manager] is very focused on the short term. He has done a good job; he has been very successful, but he drives his people wild. His operating style is that he always wants things at the last minute, and we have no choice but to do what he wants when he wants it."

Even flagging the need for time or resources up front does not seem to prevent crises from developing. Until work achieves crisis status, engineers claim they cannot attract managers' attention; requests that might prevent future crises are ignored. This

---

[1] In this chapter, I describe what sociologists call the "socio-temporal order" (Zerubaval 1979) of the Ditto product development team. On September 10, when the team committed to a product launch date of June 20, a schedule was put in place which stipulated completion dates for each of the major steps in the product's development—a temporal framework. Work, I found, tends to intensify before major deadlines and, to some extent, before minor deadlines, but the intensity of the work is perpetually high because of all the crises.

phenomenon is poignantly illustrated by one engineer's attempt to purchase some necessary software support. Jane was supposed to work with a new software program, but management refused to make a $5,000 investment for the support line that went with it. Consequently, Jane was forced to write code using a program with which she was unfamiliar and without the resources that would have enabled her to learn it quickly. The issue of purchasing the help line arose in August when Jane first recognized that she needed help. For four months, Jane asked for the resources to purchase the help line. She continued to slip farther and farther behind schedule. Eventually, Laura, her boss, asked Jane to spend the next month documenting her need for the support line. With sufficient documentation Laura felt that she would be able to convince her manager of the need to invest the money. Jane reacted to this plan with outrage. "We need it now," she exclaimed. "The amount of time I am wasting is worth more than the $5,000. A month from now, we will not need the help. It will be too late. We need it now."

Jane knew that ultimately she would be to blame if she were not able to finish on time. No one would remember that she had not been provided with sufficient support. Management would only notice that she had not completed her work. Lacking the authority to solve the problem, she felt helpless, and her frustration escalated.

In early November, Laura found a way to get Jane access to a different type of help line, but the response time was very long, often taking days. Jane explained, "The help line I have access to now takes forever. If you ask a question incorrectly, you automatically lose a whole day. We don't have that type of time to lose." Jane sent the help line her first question on a Thursday. She did not receive a response until the following Tuesday, and the first answer was not correct. She had to rephrase the question and resubmit it. Finally, on Wednesday she obtained an answer that addressed her question. At this point, Laura agreed that the current solution was inadequate. Two weeks later, in early December, Jane finally got the help line she had originally asked for in August.

According to Jane, had the relevant decision makers at Ditto spent the money four months earlier, they could have saved her trouble and wasted time. Instead, management delayed spending the money until her situation became desperate. Moreover, when they finally purchased the help line, the return on their investment was minimal. By December, Jane had spent a great deal of time figuring out most of the problems that the help line could have solved quickly.

Jane's case represents a familiar pattern for those I studied. Action is delayed until a situation becomes an emergency. When an issue becomes urgent, resources, both monetary and human, are suddenly directed toward its resolution. Often, however, it is too late to solve the problem. One engineer gave an apt analogy: "You cannot get nine women together and have a baby in one month. And yet, that is how we operate around here. We never have the resources until the last minute. Once something becomes a crisis then we throw everything at it, but by then it is often too late."[2]

Both because engineers are constantly faced with new and urgent requests and because they perceive that managers will not engage until the work becomes a crisis, engineers do not seem to plan ahead. They constantly work reactively rather than proactively.[3] When a problem becomes a crisis, it captures everyone's undivided attention, but until that time, task completion is delayed, and no time is spent preventing future crises. As a result, the future, just like the present, is unplanned, unstructured, and crisis-ridden.

As each deadline approaches, the engineers feel that it is the most important one of the project. Once it has passed, engineers expect their anxiety levels to decrease, but this never seems to occur. When I arrived in September, the engineers said November would be the worst month of the project and after Thanksgiving the situation would improve. After Thanksgiving, they believed

---

[2] Frederick P. Brooks's (1982) data substantiate this engineer's claim that waiting until the last minute and then throwing everything at problems often does not work effectively. Brooks found that adding manpower at the end of a project may actually produce the reverse of the intended effect. He showed that beyond a certain optimal number of staff, the time needed for product development *increases* rather than decreases with the addition of more "men."

[3] Steven C. Wheelwright and Kim B. Clark (1992) refer to reactive management as "after-the-fact problem solving." They note that "managers fail to plan sufficiently in advance. . . . Rather, managers often seek to respond to problems as their importance becomes apparent; at that point they are unavoidable" (p. 32).

Christmas would bring relief. After Christmas, they said things would slow down after January. This pattern continued throughout the entire development cycle as engineers constantly battled crises at work.

Effects on the Product's Development

Management initially sets deadlines to ensure timely delivery of a high-quality product. These deadlines, however, often create crisis situations, with high costs for the product. Much effort ends up directed at circumventing the deadlines, rather than producing the best product in the shortest time. The engineers I studied spent much time creating "work-arounds," patching problems with temporary solutions. These work-arounds either create more work in the end because "real solutions" are still needed, or worse, become permanent parts of the final product by default.

Moreover, when engineers work long hours to resolve crises they are prone to mistakes. Martin C. Moore-Ede (1993) reports that the *Exxon Valdez* oil spill, the Chernobyl disaster, and the explosion of the *Challenger* space shuttle all resulted from human fatigue. He finds: "Fatigued people make errors. . . . Fatigued people also work more slowly and less effectively. They do things the long and routine way, and fail to see efficient shortcuts that could be used. They do not pay attention: vats boil over, tanks overfill, tools drop into machines, and goods drop off vehicles" (p. 69).

Imagine a farmer with a wagon full of apples. He stops at the side of the road to ask how far it is to market. He is told, "If you go slow it will take you an hour, but if you go fast it will take you all day." The paradox is easily explained. If the farmer goes fast, he will hit a bump in the road, his apples will fall out, and he will then have to spend all day gathering them. The analogy with the Ditto product development process is all too apparent. If each task did not become a crisis, the engineers would have more time to solve problems as they arose. Instead, because everything is left until the last minute, routine problems often become crises, and tasks take longer than they otherwise would.

Frederick P. Brooks (1982) provides a similar analogy:

> Observe that for the programmer, as for the chef, the urgency of the patron may govern the scheduled completion of the task, but it cannot govern the actual completion. An omelette, promised in two minutes, may appear to be progressing nicely. But when it has not set in two minutes, the customer has had two choices—wait or eat it raw. Software customers have the same choices. The cook has another choice; he can turn up the heat. The result is often an omelette nothing can save—burned in one part, raw in another. (p. 21)

The engineers, like the chef, confront deadlines. When a problem needs to be solved immediately, rather than as part of the daily routine, the response tends to be haphazard and often less effective than it otherwise might be.[4]

Effects on the Engineers

Lack of planning and the resulting crises create immense work pressure for the engineers as well. Some engineers thrive in this environment. Most become overwhelmed. According to one engineer, "My life is so out of control, I feel like I have been hit by a truck." Another complained, "I cannot take it any more. We are always putting out fires. You'd think we were in the emergency room. We act like someone is dying. In reality, we're the one's who are slowly dying."

The pressure experienced by product developers and the consequences are well documented. A *New York Times* article of December 12, 1993, described the development work on the Newton by Apple Computer: "The pressure to finish, exhilarating at first, eventually overwhelmed some of the young designers. After

---

[4] I do not explore the possibility that crises energize individuals and work gets done more efficiently as a result. Engineers never suggested that to be the case, but it certainly is possible, especially given what we know about the role of deadlines. Regardless, the collaborative experiment described in Chapter 10 indicates that the negative effects of this way of working outweigh any positive ones that may exist.

eighteen-hour days, some engineers went home and cried. Some quit. One had a breakdown and ended up in jail. One took a pistol and killed himself."

In *The Soul of a New Machine,* Tracy Kidder describes a similar world of tight schedules, missed deadlines, and sleepless nights as a group of engineers battled time, corporate intrigue, and low odds to bring their technological dream to life. Before these engineers were offered jobs, they were warned, "It's gonna be a real hard job with a lot of long hours" (p. 66). Once they were in the group, the engineers went through an initiation process known as "signing up": "By signing up for the project you agreed to do whatever was necessary for success. You agreed to forsake, if necessary, family, hobbies and friends—if you had any of these left (and you might not if you had signed up too many times before)" (p. 63). Group membership required engineers to do everything possible to develop the product on time—including working overtime for no extra pay and sacrificing family life.

The time pressure seems to have been no less severe for the engineers at Tech, the high technology organization that Gideon Kunda describes in his ethnography *Engineering Culture,* or for the software engineers developing Microsoft's Windows NT as described by G. Pascal Zachary in *Showstopper.* The same pattern exists at Ditto. Every day engineers are required to arrive early and stay late to put out fires. It is an odd night when an engineer goes home early. In general, engineers leave the office when their work is completed or it is simply too late and they find themselves too tired to continue. There is no regularity to their work patterns. Only those who have what the engineers call "hard stops" regularly leave at a set time. "Hard stops" are family and school obligations that are viewed by peers and managers as unbendable or nonnegotiable. Setting hard stops, however, is an indication that the engineer puts life outside of work above work, and those who do so risk negative career consequences.

Members of the organization commonly hold that they as a group must race to get the product to market. Moreover, they are always behind schedule. There is never time to prepare for deadlines. Each deadline is confronted only when it is around the corner and has become a crisis. While engineers are busy addressing the most recent crisis, the work that they intend to do on any given day is delayed until it too is perceived as a crisis. Because engineers continuously confront crises, they have little time to invest in future work. Their ability to prevent future crises is negated. As a result, both engineers and their work suffer.

In such a world it is not surprising that individual output, willingness to accommodate to the demands of the work, and visibility at work are rewarded. Those who stay around and solve the crises become "heroes" and at least for some in the organization, role models. Faced with so many crises, however, most engineers perceive that they have little or no time to help others. Behavior like Sarah's results. Engineers end up continually interrupting others. No one can get his or her own work done, and crises perpetuate. Chapter 8 concludes Part II with a discussion of the vicious cycle that is set in motion.

8

Vicious Work Time Cycle: A Major Impediment to Corporate Productivity

The pervasive pattern of interruptions (described in Chapter 6) perpetuates the crisis mentality (described in Chapter 7) and, in turn, reinforces the assumption that long hours and a willingness to accommodate to the demands of the work are necessary to succeed (first described in Chapter 3). What I refer to as the "vicious work time cycle" is therefore set in motion (see Figure 5).[1] By rewarding individual output and presence, managers promote a way of using time which devalues helping and promotes interruptions. Without calculating and comparing costs and benefits of different work styles, managers encourage engineers to do whatever it takes to get the job done. Engineers act as if their own work is top priority and feel justified in interrupting whomever they need whenever they feel it is necessary. The result is constant interruptions, less time to accomplish "real engineering," and no appreciation for the positive role of helpful interactions. Instead, interactions are perceived as interruptions that deter the engineers from accomplishing their real engineering. This pervasive pattern of interruptions perpetuates the crisis mentality and the criteria perceived as necessary for both individual and corporate success.

---

[1] I elaborate on the implications of this finding for organization theory in Perlow 1996.

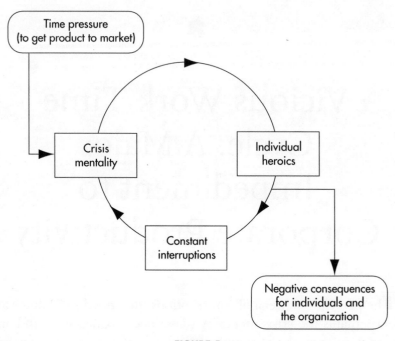

FIGURE 5
The vicious work time cycle

Since the assumptions that govern how time at work is used are never articulated or questioned, there are no incentives to be more efficient or to be more conscientious about taking up others' time. Rather, engineers continue to interrupt each other and suffer from others' tendencies to do likewise. The definition of success is self-fulfilling because in times of crisis, individual heroics are perceived as necessary to meet rapidly approaching deadlines. Yet, rewarding individual heroics promotes a disruptive way of working, which reinforces the crisis mentality and the need for individual heroics.

Individuals trapped in this cycle do "whatever it takes" to get the job done because that is the approach that promotes their individual success. Yet, their very attempts to succeed at work perpetuate a way of working which is disruptive and reinforces the crisis mentality, requiring individuals to put extraordinary amounts of time into their work.[2] In the end, because each individual is concerned with his or her own success, everyone must work harder than necessary, and neither the work itself nor individuals' lives outside of work benefit.[3]

Even for the engineers who are single, like Max, the process is draining. They continue to work this way because they feel they have no choice if they desire to succeed, but they are not content. When I returned for a brief visit six months after PEARL launched, Max said: "They keep pushing us to do it better and faster. The newness wears off. We did it the first time. We set the benchmark. Now they just want more from us in less time. Enough is enough."

Perhaps most revealing is the fact that six months after PEARL launched, the product manager himself was looking for a new job within the company. He had proved that he could manage an on-time launch, and now he wanted to take on yet another challenge. What goes unnoticed is the lack of investment he made in his people along the way. He pushed them beyond their limits and now he wanted to move on, leaving behind him a demoralized and, in the phrase of the day, "burned-out" group. The product manager took the short-term approach characteristic of almost everything at Ditto. His goal was to get the most out of his people during a particular product cycle. He would be gone during the next cycle, and what happened then would not affect his career. In fact, if the team failed after his departure, he might even look better. Some would think that he achieved what the next manager could not.

Certainly, when individuals become deeply absorbed in their work there are benefits. First and foremost, the organization benefits from the extreme dedication of its employees. Engineers

---

[2] In the late 1970s several sociologists of work indicated that individuals' acceptance of their current situation perpetuates their own oppression (i.e., Braverman 1974; Burawoy 1979; Edwards 1979). Such acceptance also characterizes the vicious work time cycle. The engineers accept the criteria for success as fair because they assume that long hours and individual heroics are the only way for them as a group to compete in a global market. By accepting these demands on their time and acting accordingly, they end up perpetuating these demands.

[3] Renee M. Landes, James O. Rebitzer, and Lowell J. Taylor (1994) refer to a specific case of this problem as the "long hours trap." They suggest that when professionals work in groups, teams, or partnerships in which all members of the group share in the outcome of other group members there is an incentive to screen out new members based on hours. The norm persists even when it does not serve the best interest of those involved.

also benefit from jobs that engage them because time at work flies by and many experience a sense of self-fulfillment. There is a dark side to this way of working, however, and not just for the engineers. My findings indicate that the costs of rewarding individual heroics and relentless hard work may far exceed the benefits.

As described in the Introduction, researchers on work/life conflicts have documented the negative effects of long hours of work on both individuals and their families. Yet, when researchers study individuals' ways of working, the criteria for success are lauded; their negative effects never mentioned. For example, Tracy Kidder (1981) describes with awe the intensity with which software engineers battle the impossible. He portrays the crisis mentality as a source of incredible excitement. Emergencies make the engineers feel needed. They stay at work to get the job done, giving the project their unwavering devotion.

Like Kidder, I find that a crisis mentality results in long work hours, but my findings indicate that it also perpetuates a definition of success which impedes achievement of business goals and reduces the ability of individuals to establish a comfortable and satisfying home life. In times of crisis, managers know of no viable option but to throw time at problems. Moreover, managers value individual heroics that pull the team through. Consequently, engineers learn to concentrate on their own deliverables above all else, single-mindedly pursuing anything they need for their own work. The result is that they constantly interrupt each other, no one gets enough work done, and further crises develop. Because everyone is busy responding to crises no one has time to prevent future crises. The vicious cycle keeps on spinning. Deadlines are always too close and the product is not ready by the scheduled date. The hard work that crises inspire may seem desirable to managers, but the negative effects of this way of working should not be ignored. In Part III, I further explore these effects and the potential for change.

PART III

The Possibility of Change

We can conclude that the current way of using time has detrimental consequences for individuals and families. It also appears to have negative effects for the corporation. It remains to be considered, however, whether the costs to the corporation indeed exceed the benefits. If it turns out that changing the way of using time improves productivity, then we will be able to conclude that the current costs outweigh the benefits.

In Part III, I address several questions: Is change possible? Would change be desirable? And who would benefit from change? First, I examine the attempts of individuals to change their own work patterns. I focus on the implementation of flexible work options, such as flextime, flexplace, job sharing and part-time work. These policies, permitting employees to create alternative schedules, are the current corporate solution to employees' problems of balancing work and family responsibilities. In Chapter 9, I discuss the case of one woman who took advantage of these policies and describe the negative career consequences she suffered as a result. At the end of the chapter, I consider why these policies in particular and individual attempts in general are likely to fail in a culture like Ditto's.

In Chapter 10, I consider a collaborative attempt with the engineers collectively to restructure their way of using time at work.

The collaborative experiment I conducted serves two purposes. First, it investigates the potential for collective change and the benefits to individuals, families, and the corporation. Second, it addresses the question raised in Part II, whether the costs to the organization of the current way of using time exceed the benefits. The experiment itself is unusual for an ethnography.[1] To discover whether change is possible and whether individuals, their families, and the corporation could all benefit, it was not enough merely to observe work practices. Rather, change actually had to be attempted and the results documented.

To gather the data described in Chapter 10, I therefore combine elements of ethnography with what Edgar Schein (1987) has labeled the "clinical perspective."[2] In ethnographic research the group members participate but have no particular stake in the intellectual issues motivating the study. In contrast, in clinical research the subject's or the client's interests are the prime motivator for an outsider's involvement. The nature of the relationship differs from researcher/subject to consultant/client. Like a researcher, I was not paid by the organization and I did have my own agenda—to study the use of time and the possibility for change. Like a clinician, however, I engaged the managers and engineers as more than mere subjects with a disinterested role in my study. I brought their agendas to the surface as well as my own.[3]

Our shared objective was to find out if we could make changes in the engineers' work practices which would enhance both their work/family balance and their work productivity. We

---

[1] Ethnography refers to both a method (fieldwork) and its subject (culture). The ethnographer starts with the assumption that the organization is there to be understood. She goes to a location for an extended period of time, "living with and living like" the people studied. When the fieldwork is complete, the ethnographer interprets the data to see what has been learned and decides how to present it. The ethnographer's ultimate goal is to create a cultural representation of the world as observed (Van Maanen 1988).

[2] The clinical perspective is based on an action research model. One begins with the assumption that one cannot understand a human system without trying to change it (Lewin 1948). For the clinician, intervention precedes or is simultaneous with diagnosis. The primary source of data is not what is "out there" to be observed but what is learned while working with the client to create change. The clinician's ultimate goal is to create a model or theory that makes it possible to predict the results of a given intervention (Schein 1987).

[3] Lotte Bailyn and the other members of the larger team conducting the Ford Foundation study of which this project was a part have labeled this method of intertwining research and intervention "collaborative interactive action research" (Bailyn et al. 1996).

were engaged together in questioning old assumptions, considering alternatives to accepted work practices, and designing needed changes. Chapter 10 is devoted to our collaborative experiment. The book concludes in Chapter 11 with a discussion of the benefits of restructuring time use for individuals, families, and the corporation.

9

Flexible Work Options Fall Short: Kate's Story

Ditto engineers have "ad hoc flexibility."[1] In other words, they can come and go each day as they choose. There are no official starting times, departure times, or required working hours for a given week. Crises that occur outside of work can usually be accommodated without a struggle. A dentist appointment, a flat tire, or a sick child does not pose a problem. What does create a problem is an individual's unwillingness to put work first on a regular basis. In general, family needs are not to take precedence over work. Those individuals who want to be successful at work cannot expect to go home at a scheduled time each day and to work late only occasionally to cope with a crisis. Rather, the expectation is reversed: people must work late regularly, and occasionally arrive home at a decent hour (usually because of a family crisis).

In theory Ditto offers its employees a wide array of flexible options, including flextime, flexplace, job sharing, and part-time work, to give them a choice about how they balance home demands with work demands. Indeed, Robert Levering and Milton Moskowitz list Ditto in their book *The 100 Best Companies to Work for in America*. The company is also on *Working Mother*'s list of the top one hundred places for women to work. According to *Money*

---

[1] Deborah Kolb coined this term.

Magazine (June 1, 1992), Ditto's benefit package is among the ten best in America.

Yet, the engineers at Ditto express surprise when they hear such facts about their company. They insist it is impossible to take advantage of any of the flexible work options without hindering their career advancement. As one woman said, "You really cannot leave for a few months and come back and expect to get to high levels. You have to be recommended for a manager's job. And so people look back at your record and see if you are committed, if you were willing to put the time in. And if not, well, you don't go anywhere." Another female engineer simply stated, "It is like a train. . . . if you get off, you can't get back on. It is a real problem."

In the end, individuals struggling to balance work and family find themselves with no real options to manage both successfully. Despite the good intentions behind flexible work policies, employees who take advantage of them tend to suffer career consequences (e.g., Shamir and Salomon 1985; Leidner 1988; Perin 1991). Kate's case reveals both the potential gains from flexible work schedules and the way individuals' attempts to utilize such options are currently undermined.

Kate's Case

Kate, a member of the PEARL software group, opted to work at home one day a week to help juggle her career, her three young children, and her 2½-hour commute.[2] After eight months of taking advantage of this option, however, she was assigned a new job working with confidential data that could not leave the lab. Consequently, Kate could no longer work at home. She described the problem with her new job: "It isn't just that I cannot work from home. It is boring and unchallenging work and I don't see the value in it even once I am done. If at least I saw the value, I would feel like it was less demoralizing." To make matters worse, over

---

[2] One should keep in mind that Kate was married to Pete, who set limits on the amount he would do at home and said they would have a fight if Kate was not home on time.

the course of the year, Kate fell from a ranking of "premium employee" to "below average employee."

Kate's managers claimed that the quality of her work declined in her new job, and perhaps it did, but the question is why they assigned her this new position. Kate, as well as many of her peers (and even some Ditto managers), believed that she was given this work as punishment for trying to accommodate her schedule to her family's needs. The managers responsible for giving her the poor performance rating, however, said this job assignment was important work that she failed to complete adequately. They took no responsibility for not clarifying the importance of the work, nor did they provide any explanation for why a premium employee would suddenly not be able to perform up to the organization's standards.

The history of her case unfolded as follows. From January to August 1993 (the eight months before my study began), Kate's managers viewed her as a "successful" project leader of a team of six engineers. Kate spoke with pride when she described this role, "I took what they considered to be a difficult group . . . individuals who were notorious for not getting along, and I created a self-managed work team. I know it is an important skill to be able to empower a team like this." Because Kate created a self-managed team, she was able to work at home one day a week, saving herself a long commute and increasing the amount of uninterrupted time she had to work on her individual deliverables.[3] Kate found working at home very productive. "I could get more than two days' worth of work done in one, and still have time left over for educational advancement, reading manuals, and more."[4]

---

[3] Kate's husband is ten years older than she and teaches in a public middle school two and a half hours from Ditto. He cannot change school districts without giving up his seniority. When Kate was looking for work three and a half years ago, the best job she could find was at Ditto. In an attempt to accommodate both of their careers, they live with their three children in a small town close to the midpoint between their workplaces. Kate commutes one hour and fifteen minutes each way, every day.

[4] It is important to note that Kate's productivity at home was based only on completing real engineering, not interactive work. For this type of software engineering, working at home can only be optimal up to a point because interactions have been found to play a critical role in the work process. Nevertheless, as will become evident in Chapter 10, the optimal scenario involves blocks of uninterrupted individual time. Essentially, by working at home one day a week, Kate modeled a version of this temporal structure.

Not only did Kate benefit because she could work at home, but so did her engineers, who were able to learn about managing a project and experience what it means to be empowered. To accommodate her working at home, Kate invented a rotating position of acting manager, which her engineers took turns filling. She commented, "This provided them good exposure to what the role of a manager was like." According to one of her engineers, "I really enjoyed working for Kate. I had the opportunity to take on responsibility I would not typically have had at my level. This made me more aware of what managers do." Another of her engineers reflected, "After working for Kate I have a better understanding of what it means to manage. I attended meetings I would never have otherwise been a part of." A third engineer explained, "Working for Kate we had much greater control of our work. She trusted us to make decisions for ourselves." Kate's six-month review referred to it as the "best year of her career" and noted that her group was on schedule. Her peers considered her a "rising star."

When I met Kate in September 1993 she had just been reassigned to her new job working with confidential data. Her assignment was to evaluate the most recent software release of a vendor's product. Kate believed, however, that senior management had already made up their mind. "They want to use the older, more established release. . . . they are having me investigate the newer product just to reassure themselves that they have made the right decision." According to Kate, she was in a "lose-lose situation." If she recommended use of the older version, management's response to her work would be "we told you so." On the other hand, if she advised using the upgraded version, she believed that they would not accept her recommendation. Kate was convinced that her managers were beyond influence: "They have already made up their minds and they will use the older software release, no matter what I do." She described herself as "disempowered" and maintained, "I have no say in the final decision. I do not even have any understanding of the financial implications of using one release as opposed to the other. Without any of this information, it is impossible for me to be motivated to do work that I think is worthless."

The software engineers who shared Kate's lab had similar perceptions of her situation. They thought that Kate was a "wasted resource," and they wondered aloud, "Why does management keep Kate on a project that is so pointless when she is a technically competent engineer and there is so much work to be done with the older software release?" Because the other engineers in her lab believed that her work was low priority, it was not uncommon for them to ask for her help or to borrow her computer for hours, sometimes even days. Her peers saw this behavior as "facilitating the progress of the team." Kate let this happen "because I agree with them that their work is more critical than mine."

By November Kate had become so disgruntled with her situation that she tried to leave the division. It is Ditto's policy that an employee can change jobs internally if his or her manager approves the change. Kate found a desirable position on another product team in a different division. Although she was offered the job, her manager's manager (the senior software manager) would not authorize the change. Instead, he promised Kate that her situation within the group would soon improve. He said she was being "targeted" to be a project team leader in his group. Kate expressed doubts to me whether she would even want such a job in this group, but since her manager would not sign, she had no choice but to stay. She felt, at least, that her manager's remarks indicated that he was satisfied with her performance.

By early December, Kate was so frustrated with the job that she decided to approach her manager's manager again to try to persuade him to let her change jobs. The week that she was finally ready to act, however, Ditto announced a 10 percent reduction in the work force and scheduled the first round of layoffs for mid-January. Since Kate did not want to be caught between jobs during a reduction in work force, she suspended all action to leave the group.

Before the end of December, Kate was reassigned again, this time within her own product team but reporting to a different project team leader. She now found herself working for the project team leader that, she had been told less than two months earlier, she was being groomed to replace. This time she was replacing someone who had gone on disability leave.[5] Someone had to

---

[5] At Ditto, maternity leave is categorized as a disability leave. In this case the engineer left suddenly for extended maternity leave because of medical complications.

pick up this individual's work. Kate believed her transfer was yet another indication that the work she had been doing was not important. She accepted her new assignment and tried to make the best of it. She learned quickly, meeting her deliverables and supporting her new teammates. I often found Kate sitting with her teammates in front of a computer terminal jointly trying to solve bugs in their code. I never heard Kate say who was helping whom, but, when I asked others, it was always Kate who was *giving* help.

Everything Falls Apart

When the raises for the year were announced just after her second reassignment, but based primarily on her assignment evaluating the software release that could not leave the lab, Kate received nothing. She was devastated. Six months earlier she had received the best review of her career. After two more months as project team leader, followed by four months on a low-priority, low visibility assignment, followed by yet another reassignment, she was shocked to receive no raise. When Kate received her review, she refused to sign it. "To sign it," she explained, "would indicate that I accept it, and I do not." She was upset in part because she had received no indication from her managers that they saw her performance as problematic. She had always been a top performer. She had no reason to think that things had changed. Kate said: "If the review process was working, I should have at least known that I was perceived as a problem. But I had no such indication."

Kate's initial reaction was to go into her office, close the door, and sob. She noted, "I have never before cried at work." Once she was able to compose herself, she went to her manager and demanded an explanation. Kate said her manager blamed her zero raise on a bad year: "He told me that I was in the wrong place at the wrong time. He had no further explanation."

Kate next asked her manager's manager, Zeth, to explain:

> Zeth told me that I had not statused him appropriately. Zeth claimed that I did not let him know that I was having all the problems that I was having. At that point I nearly lost it, but instead I

joked with him that clearly, "I was not communicating well." So, I went back and pulled out all my weekly status reports from the four months I was on the project. I showed him how I was busy updating him regularly. I further showed him how I had noted over and over that I was facing problems and was getting no help, no sense of direction, and no sense that what I was doing was important. . . . Beyond complaining about the lack of status, Zeth had no further explanation for why I received a zero.

Dissatisfied with Zeth's response, Kate approached his manager, and even his manager's manager. Eventually, she took her case to the division vice-president—four management levels up. She argued:

My first eight months were my best, and I had always been a premium employee, and my last four months were on an assignment of no value. . . . I am better than this and will not let them treat me this way. I know that I am marketable. I will leave if that is what it takes. It is not the money, but I will push for a salary increase because I am afraid that a zero will haunt my career for a long time. . . . The issue is what other people will think of me. And especially in the case of another layoff, I have to worry that I will be out the door if I am not careful.

When I spoke with Kate's managers, they focused on what they regarded as her "lack of commitment" over the past four months and declared that the second assignment had been a "real opportunity for Kate to prove herself." Some, however, also expressed regret. Allan, her immediate manager, said:

I never communicated the importance of the task to Kate and the vendor certainly did not think that she was going to succeed. The challenge was to demonstrate that it could be done. It was a great opportunity to become the group expert. It is not clear to me that the task could have been accomplished by anyone, but at least a star engineer would have gone down swinging. . . . I did treat it like a low-priority task. We certainly were not going to jeopardize the older release for it, and Kate certainly had some major barriers to overcome. . . . When I was at her grade level, I would have killed for the assignment. It was a great opportunity to make a contribution and acquire new skills. I was disappointed with her attitude.

Zeth, Allan's boss, made similar arguments:

The new software release would have reduced the printer cost by $300, and Kate failed. Now I have to find an alternative way to reduce cost. Her task was important. I would not have had her do it if I did not think so. We are short of resources, so obviously it was necessary to use them as best we could. I felt that the new release really did offer a possible solution to the issue of cost reduction. A superstar engineer would have succeeded. It was a challenging task, and the fact she failed does not mean that she is a bad engineer, only average. . . . The only reason I called off the effort was because Kate had provided insufficient data, and there was too great a risk to going ahead.

Kate appealed her performance review for several months. By the end, she looked exhausted. She seemed to have no enthusiasm for her work. Kate said: "I am no longer able to sleep at night, and during the day my attention is on battling for what I deserve, not on my deliverables." The incident left her bitter. One Monday morning, in the midst of the fight over her performance review, she said: "It is not fair. This is taking so much time. And I can think of nothing else. This past weekend, no matter what I was doing, I found myself thinking about how unfair this all is."

Kate's struggle finally came to an end when Milton, the product manager, approached her. According to Kate, "He said, 'Your performance reviews do not have the superlatives in them that the others have.' " Kate told me afterward, "That stuff is fluff. I never realized that I needed to make sure that there was enough fluff. But, I will be sure to do that in the future. . . . In the meeting I was very hurt and I did all that I could to hold back tears. When he asked me if I wanted to stay in the group I gave him a definitive no and added that there are no career opportunities here. And he just said, 'Okay.' " At this point, Kate was finally able to obtain a manager's approval to leave the group.

Although Milton delivered the news, he was not directly involved in the decision to deny Kate a raise. Milton told me at one point: "I never understood why Carl (the senior software manager in charge at the time) would have been pushing for the new software release. It never seemed a feasible source of cost reduction to me. I understand why Kate's heart was not in this work." Milton also said, "Any employee who drops from premium to below average in a year that they successfully managed six people for eight months, deserves to be upset." He confided, "Kate asked to work at home one day per week, and I suspect that is underlying her drop." Yet, despite these comments, Milton went along with the decision.

In July, Kate joined the division she had tried to join the previous November. Kate said, "This process has taken a toll. I will try the new group, but I am considering leaving the company." She describes herself as very cautious now: "I am on the defensive. If nothing else, this experience taught me that I have to stand up at all times for myself. I have to think of myself and my work, above all else. And I have to make sure I never get stuck on a bad assignment. I learned never to get stuck on a side project. One must always fight to be in the limelight. And I think I better be very careful about working from home, even if it seems like it is going well."

In the end, the managers involved seemed relieved when Kate decided to leave, and they never mentioned the loss the group suffered. When I asked the quality and business effectiveness manager his reaction to losing Kate, he responded, "She is leaving? Where is she going? I had no idea." He then added, "I guess that shows you how insignificant the team must think it is, if I have not even heard about it."

Constraints from Home

Kate had constraints on her work time, and she tried to devise a schedule that would benefit herself and others as well. She created a self-managed team so that she could work at home. Those in the group had an unusual opportunity to act as managers, the project did not suffer, and group members said the arrangement worked to everyone's advantage. Yet, Kate was given no recognition for her innovative way of managing. Instead, the common perception is that Kate was punished for working at home and given a new assignment on which she had almost no chance of succeeding.

The managers justified their actions by pointing to what they considered Kate's poor performance on her new job, but they also mentioned problems with her family situation. One manager said, "Home is stifling her career possibilities." Several other managers noted that Kate had once declined management training—a program that would have required her to be away from home for two weeks. They took this decision as an indication that Kate "does not make sacrifices" at home for work, and they never mentioned the special circumstances behind her decision. Kate, however, explained that the class fell in the same week that her family was to move into a new house. After discussions with her husband, she decided she could not leave them during such a chaotic period. When she declined, she requested a future "opportunity," but managers have not granted this request, nor do they ever mention it.

Among the many factors demanding Kate's time at home were her father's death during the fall and her mother's resulting financial troubles. Several weeks after finding out that she had received no raise, Kate said: "I have not been able to focus on my mother's problems, but I need to get involved. No one is handling them."

Kate also faced marital difficulties. As apparently open and honest as Kate was with me about her work life, she did not want me to interview her husband. When I asked about spouse interviews, she said, "I think it is a great idea, but in my case it will not be possible." For several months I said nothing. As I finished up the interviews in April, Kate approached me rather timidly, asked how they were going, and said offhandedly, "I think it might be okay for you to visit my house, as well." When I did visit, Kate's husband turned out to be quite vocal. He was very resentful of the demands that Ditto seemed to be putting on his wife, and therefore himself. He complained about the stress he felt Kate was under at work and the difficulties they were experiencing as they tried to cope with the demands of two careers and a growing family.

A Poignant Comparison

Laura, the project team leader described in Chapter 2, is now Kate's manager. Both are women with three children and working husbands. A year ago they were professional equals, both targeted as "rising stars." Last year, both were in their first managerial positions. The difference between them is that Laura accommodates the system and Kate challenges it. Laura never resists higher managers' requests; she tries to expand the time at work in order to avoid ever having to refuse. Kate, by contrast, turns down work that does not match the time she has available. Her work schedule is more rigid.

Kate created an innovative way to get her work done which seemed to have salutary effects on others as well, but it is Laura, *not Kate*, who is perceived as the ideal female employee. In a year that both Kate and Laura acted as project leaders for the first eight months, Laura was promoted and ranked in the top 10 percent of managers. Kate was not promoted and ranked in the bottom 20 percent of employees.

Failures such as Kate's reinforce the assumption that employees have no real options for successfully balancing work and family. Flexible work policies serve only to create a new category of workers for whom flexibility may reduce stress, but at the risk of damaging their career prospects. These individuals end up on what has come to be known as "the mommy track."

The problem is that flexible work options are offered without altering underlying assumptions about how work should be done or what it takes to succeed at work.[6] If one chooses to take advantage of these policies, one risks being seen as "different," "less committed," and "less able to perform." Efficiency and effectiveness are simply not valued to the same degree as physical presence and sacrifices in life outside of work. Without deeper cultural change to redefine these actions as "acceptable," individuals who pursue a different path risk negative consequences for not conforming.

---

[6] I elaborate on the barriers to the successful implementation of flexible work options in Perlow 1995a.

If individuals who choose to use flexible options are to have the potential of being considered loyal, committed, hardworking employees, the criteria for success will have to be modified. These criteria, however, are deeply embedded in a culture built on the notion that work should be placed above all else. Moreover, the current emphasis on speed and the perpetuation of crises only serve to reinforce the need for individuals who will put in whatever hours are required whenever they are needed. To reward alternative behavior will require breaking out of the vicious work time cycle itself.

Given the magnitude of the changes that must be made before flexible work options can be successful, it is not surprising that *individual's* attempts to create change fail, despite the potential benefits of such change for the individuals, their families, and the corporation. In the next chapter, I describe the collaborative experiment I conducted with the engineers to explore the possibility, and potential benefits, of collective change.

10

Potential
for Collective Change:
Quiet Time

Each engineer perceives stress and overwork as his or her own individual problem. As a result, engineers' responses amount to individual tradeoffs in accordance with their personal desires for organizational success and family involvement. As described in the last chapter, however, individual accommodation of family responsibilities hinders one's organizational success and perpetuates the assumption that change is not possible.

But what if the difficulties experienced by individuals were reframed as a systemic or organizational problem? I devised a field experiment to examine the assumption that existing work patterns are necessary and inflexible. My hypothesis was that work could be redesigned to make it easier for employees to get their jobs done, minimize crises, and thus reduce the need for excessively long work hours.

After I had been on site full-time for four months, I asked the engineers to reflect on what about work makes it difficult to integrate work and personal life. At first, they told me that pressure to work long hours was the issue. Yet, when I suggested limiting their work hours, they expressed great resistance, claiming that they could not possibly get their work done in less time. When I pushed them for reasons, it became clear that constant interruptions force them to work long hours to get their jobs done. Individuals who

have responsibilities outside of work are acutely aware of the consequences of this problem. The perpetuation of constant interruptions also affects the product development process itself, however.
These effects were not as apparent to the members of the organization. I therefore engaged the engineers in a collective attempt to use
their time shortage as a catalyst for change that would both benefit
the private lives of the engineers *and facilitate achievement of the corporation's business goals.*

After conversations with each of the seventeen members of the
software group, I convened a meeting and proposed to the group,
as well as the project manager and the division vice-president,
an experiment during which members of the group would be left
uninterrupted for blocks of "quiet time" during the day. The purpose was to see if alternative, less disruptive ways of working
might enable people to accomplish more during customary business hours.

It is important to note that the purpose of the proposed
change was not to minimize interactions. On the contrary, I
hoped to optimize both individual time and interactive time.
When interactions are scattered throughout the day they are perceived as interruptions, but if they could be given a set time of
their own, their value might be recognized. In other words, underlying the attempt to provide individuals with quiet time to get
their own work done, was an interest in creating alternative times
for those interactions essential to the work process.

Prior to temporally restructuring their work, the engineers
came in early, stayed late, and worked weekends trying to avoid
interruptions. The changes were designed to place some of this
precious quiet time within the normal work day. It was hoped
that this change would reduce the hours individuals had to work
as well as lead to a more effective way of working which would
benefit the corporation in a number of ways including shorten-
ing the product's development cycle.

As I worked with the group to refine the proposal, several
problems surfaced. The first involved the definition of a "legiti-
mate violation." One engineer told another: "We need to have
an open mind in order to do this experiment, and only if the
roof caves in should there be an interruption." He continued,

"We need to do this to learn and be able to analyze the situation." Another engineer wondered, "What about walking down the hall? How do you deal with interruptions then?" A peer responded, "You tell them you are in quiet time. There is no way to have perfect quiet time, but let's give it a try." Eventually the group decided that the rule would be as follows: "If the person you need to talk to were in a meeting, but you feel your interruption is important enough that you would interrupt the meeting to speak to that person, then and only then, your interruption is important enough to cause a violation of quiet time." The operational goal of the experiment was to achieve zero violations of this rule.

Engineers and managers also voiced concern about the timing of the proposed experiment. It was the middle of January and, come the end of January, the team would shift from the design phase to the testing phase. Many felt that during the testing phase interactions would be critical and quiet time would be more problematic. Initially, we agreed to limit quiet time to two and a half weeks, thus keeping it within the design phase, but quiet time was so successful that it continued for several months into the testing phase. In the end, engineers and managers told me that they learned that interactions *can* wait, regardless of the phase of the product's development.

A third problem related to the time of day. The software manager proposed quiet time between 10 A.M. and 2 P.M. He felt that after the Sunrise meeting he needed to be able to meet with the engineers, so that they would be working on the "high-priority items" for the day. He also wanted the opportunity to "check in" with them at night before they went home to learn of their progress. Several of the engineers reminded him that the goal of quiet time was to avoid labeling tasks as critical. They argued that it was not in their best interest to have their manager shift their priorities every morning especially because their priorities would often shift back by afternoon. The software manager maintained his position. He argued, "We must go along with the existing process or it won't work." But the engineers, with my support, kept challenging their manager, and eventually he agreed to try quiet time in the morning.

Phase 1

The team established Phase 1 of the study, setting quiet time three days a week. Quiet time would end at noon, but no starting time was set. We wanted to avoid any explicit determination of when people were to arrive at work. The three days chosen were Tuesday, Thursday, and Friday. Engineers felt that Monday was a particularly busy morning, which required responses to those crises that had emerged in the testing lab over the weekend. Since these crises tended to involve people beyond the software group, the engineers decided not to have quiet time on Monday mornings.

The engineers were willing to experiment with quiet time because they were eager to have the uninterrupted time to complete their work. Managers, however, were worried. They did not want to be involved in any changes that might slow the team down. A conditional rule was therefore established: If anyone became distressed, the project would be halted immediately.

With teamwide commitment, the study began. Late each evening before days with quiet time, I hung up signs around the office and on the lab doors. For example, on January 25 the sign read:

TODAY:
Quiet Time
until 12 P.M.
Tuesday 1/25

I also left a sign on each engineer's chair to remind him or her of quiet time and to be displayed by the engineer at a place of his or her choosing to remind others.

After the first phase of quiet time ended, I asked the seventeen individuals involved to fill out a brief questionnaire in which they rated their productivity in comparison to their productivity prior to the experiment, both overall and during quiet time blocks. Nearly 60 percent of the engineers said that their general productivity was "above average" (4 or 5 on a scale of 1–5). Slightly more

(65 percent) said their productivity during quiet time was "above average" (4 or 5 on a scale of 1–5).

Written comments on the questionnaire were of two types. The first was indications that quiet time provided an opportunity to address work that the engineer would otherwise have been unable to complete. One wrote, "There was an expectation that I would have certain hours to complete an individual task—I planned on it and it actually got done. I am not usually able to accomplish this when there is no quiet time." Another noted, "Uninterrupted periods of time enable me to do some of the activities during the day which I would have normally deferred to late evening."

The second type of response indicated that quiet time forced the software engineers to change their behavior during nonquiet periods as well. The engineers wrote that they now thought about interruptions and postponed them when possible, even when it was not quiet time. For example, one engineer noted, "It helped me organize work in more productive ways. Helped my self-discipline in terms of forcing me to try to solve problems or find the answer before interrupting another engineer." Another noted, "It generally made me think about making any interruption first, much more than before."

Phase 2

After the first two and a half weeks, the group met again. At this point, I suggested an alternative structure, making interaction time, not quiet time, the central focus. I proposed that in the second phase they set aside blocks of time specifically for interaction. Managers liked this idea, as they were interested in improving communication among the engineers, especially across the full product team, not just within the software group. The software group had a reputation for not being helpful to other members of the product team. Interaction time would provide the members of the larger team with a fixed period when they knew they could approach the software group and get responses to their questions.

I was also concerned that too much quiet time would diminish interaction. After all, emphasis on quiet time did not challenge the underlying assumption about the importance of individual deliverables above all else. Quiet time could be perceived as merely an opportunity for engineers to get their real engineering done, whereas focusing on interaction time would, I hoped, reveal the importance of communication. If there was a period when the engineers were encouraged to interact, perhaps they would rethink their interactions and come to recognize their value in the product development process.

The group agreed to try "interaction time," but again, timing was an issue. The software manager wanted to "put interactive time in the morning in the second phase. . . . Priorities are shifting daily and there needs to be a means to communicate them early in the day." When we voted, however, the engineers preferred to try interactive time in the middle of the day, keeping early mornings for quiet time. Reluctantly, the software manager agreed to go along. In Phase 2 interaction time was set from 11 A.M. to 3 P.M. By default, this made the period before 11 A.M. and after 3 P.M. quiet time. This schedule was to operate every weekday.[1]

This phase of the study was less effective. Almost from the moment it started, engineers complained.[2] As the first few individuals broke the rules about when they could and could not interact, the remainder had incentive to follow their lead. The new temporal structure was only minimally adhered to during its run of two and a half weeks.

The fact that the signs were not changed every day probably affected adherence to the structure. In the second phase, there

---

[1] In retrospect, it is clear to me that having interaction time five days a week was problematic. I should not have agreed to alter two variables at once. Interaction time should have been on the same three days as quiet time. The engineers, however, were caught up in the excitement over their experience with quiet time and wanted to expand it to five days a week. I had a different agenda. I wanted to explore interaction time as opposed to quiet time. Since it was a collaborative project, I agreed to do both, but altering two variables makes it difficult to decipher exactly what went on.

[2] Interestingly, engineers complained that there was *too much* quiet time, rarely that there was too little interaction time. From the start, they focused on the quiet time surrounding interaction time as opposed to the interaction time itself. Interaction time is not consistent with their assumptions about how they do their work. The idea of encouraging interactions seems to have been uncomfortable for a group whose members strive to minimize their interactions.

were no special dates involved, since every day was quiet time. A daily change of signs therefore seemed unnecessary. For the whole period, the office walls displayed the same signs:

Every day this week
Interaction time
11 A.M.–3 P.M.
Quiet Time
Before 11 A.M. and After 3 P.M.

As a result, there was no longer a continual reminder that a study promoting a different approach to work was under way.

At the end of the second phase, I again distributed a questionnaire asking engineers about their reactions. The self-rating data make it evident that there was a decline in perceived productivity gains achieved during the first phase. Overall, 47 percent of the engineers felt that the imposed temporal structure enhanced their productivity, down from 59 percent in Phase 1. In terms of productivity during quiet time, 59 percent of the engineers felt that their productivity was above average, down from 65 percent in Phase 1. Moreover, 6 percent of the engineers now felt quiet time actually hindered their productivity, whereas none had felt this way during Phase 1.

The engineers' written comments about Phase 2 mirrored their survey responses. One engineer wrote, "I did not obey quiet time as well as in Phase 1. Too much of it probably." Another noted, "It was too restrictive. Everyone just gave up because of this. So there really was only a little quiet time in the morning." Some comments suggested that engineers preferred one long block of quiet time to the two we were trying. Several individuals commented that "the time was too broken up, causing more violations."

Most respondents seemed to have overlooked the endorsement of interaction which was the purpose of Phase 2. One engineer noted, "I liked the notion of interaction time as an opportunity to foster and build communication." In general, however, the engineers did not mention improvement in the quality of their interactions, as had been hoped.

The questionnaire data substantiate my impression that the second phase was not as effective as the first. Nevertheless, it is important to note that a large percentage of the engineers still found the imposed temporal structure productive. Over half of the engineers mentioned general benefits that they felt derived from having some temporal structure imposed on their day.

The greater success of Phase 1 compared to Phase 2 implies that it may be easier to eliminate interactions during certain parts of the day than it is to schedule them into parts of the day. This difference poses several questions. Why is it that quiet time was sacred during Phase 1 but not in Phase 2? What was it about the second phase that made it less effective? Was it indeed, as engineers thought, that there was too much quiet time and that Phase 2 was too restrictive? Or could it be that the novelty of the experiment had worn off, and individuals were simply no longer motivated to participate?

Phase 3

In order to answer some of these questions, I repeated Phase 1 of the study as Phase 3. Again, for two and a half weeks, quiet time was imposed three days a week until noon. Again I posted dated signs on the office walls, and again I distributed signs the evening before to remind the engineers. After two and a half weeks, the engineers filled out another questionnaire, and again there was enthusiasm about quiet time. No one found that the imposed structure hurt their productivity, and 65 percent felt that it enhanced their productivity, up from 47 percent in the second phase and even slightly up from the 59 percent in the first phase. The same pattern appeared in the individuals' assessments of their productivity during quiet time. In Phase 3, 71 percent of the engineers described their productivity as above average during quiet time compared to 59 percent in Phase 2 and 65 percent in Phase 1.

The increase in the number of engineers who said quiet time enhanced their productivity may indicate that the effects are cumulative. In the first phase, the engineers had not yet had the chance to practice planning ahead and postponing interruptions. During the first phase engineers spoke of their "struggle to prepare for quiet time." Problems developed when they discovered they were not well prepared to work alone and needed help from a colleague to continue. Often what they needed was something that they could easily have prepared ahead of time, but they were not used to thinking ahead. As effective as they found the first phase, it was still new to them. By the third phase, however, they were accustomed to having uninterrupted time and therefore were able to prepare more effectively for noninteractive periods.

Many comments on the survey testified to a general preference for Phase 3 over Phase 2. One dominant theme was that there was less quiet time in Phase 3, and therefore, people treated it as a "precious commodity" to be treasured and respected. One engineer explained, "Phase 3 was less restrictive and it seemed like everyone took it more seriously because there was less time. Maybe Phase 2 was not taken as seriously because there was almost 'too much' quiet time." Another engineer suggested, "The non-quiet time [in Phase 2] conflicted with lunch. So, the interaction time was sometimes disrupted by the thought of going to lunch. That left little time for interaction and consequently the quiet time was violated." One engineer articulated the issue quite succinctly, "Phase 3 is much better. It is a more focused, shorter time and less violations result."

Some engineers, however, stressed that they preferred Phase 3 not so much because there was less quiet time but because it occurred in one continuous block. One wrote, "I prefer Phase 3. It provides an uninterrupted block of time during the morning." Another engineer expressed similar views, "Phase 3 is better since it provides one continuous time interval for critical design and development activity." A third noted, "Phase 3 seemed to work better since it did not split up the day into awkward time blocks."

Beyond noting that Phase 3 was preferable, several engineers highlighted the general benefits of quiet time. One commented, "I believe people have begun to respect others' work time. The focus has moved from themselves to the team. Interruptions still occur, but people take the time to think about what they are doing before interrupting. They are more prepared." Another engineer said, "It seems changes need to be mostly cultural. The idea that every problem has urgency must change. Not only does the immediate interruption of others, because the problem needs attention right now, hurt the people that are interrupted, but communication suffers because it is done so haphazardly. . . . Now we are beginning to think problems through, decide who can help, and communicate to all that need to know."

The software manager, who had been so skeptical at the outset of the experiment, particularly of the idea of morning quiet time, proclaimed, "It does not matter when we have quiet time. I have come to realize interactions can wait. . . . Quiet time enables me to do work I used to have to do in the evening, and now I am able to get it done at work. . . . quiet time has enabled me to get rid of a lot of unproductive things I used to do that were unnecessary."

Self-Managed Quiet Time

After three phases, the enthusiasm for quiet time was high among the software group. Many admitted that their initial skepticism was unfounded. Most wanted to continue. The software engineers therefore decided to try to institutionalize it. There was no change in the reward structure, just a collective agreement to continue quiet time on a three-day schedule, just as in Phase 1 and Phase 3. I was no longer involved in monitoring quiet time or in debriefing the engineers. I was present for the next month, however, and I noted a marked deterioration in the engineers' adherence to quiet time. Many engineers spoke favorably of the study and what they had learned. Yet, quiet time as previously structured began to disintegrate.

A month after Phase 3 ended, I gave the engineers one final questionnaire, about "self-managed quiet time." Fewer individuals felt that their general productivity was above what it had been prior to the project. Still, 47 percent of the engineers indicated that their productivity was higher than average, and 53 percent felt that quiet time was more productive than their normal work time. The comments on the survey supported my sense that the temporal structure created by quiet time was no longer strictly followed. One engineer noted, "Quiet time has not been observed, it needs to be enforced." Another said, "There still needs to be more done before quiet time will become institutionalized." In general, however, the software engineers seemed pleased with the lessons they learned from the study and the effects the experience were still having on the group. One engineer explained: "We have not been adhering to any quiet time guidelines, but I believe the general level of productivity is up. People are much more sensitive to others' rights to have 'quiet-time,' and there is definite change in behavior patterns, I think primarily due to quiet time." Another said, "There are less interruptions now even though there is no official quiet time." Still another said, "Interruptions occur when they need to, after preparation." And another wrote, "People are more respectful of others' time, people plan to work together versus expecting an immediate response. Managers don't expect immediate attention either. People are more relaxed." One engineer summed it up: "I think everyone is more considerate of other people's work loads, and people are trying to plan around each other better. I think everyone is more considerate about interrupting. I think a lot of the rules concerning quiet time are more ingrained."

After a month of "self-managed quiet time," we had one last meeting at which I presented the data I had collected over all four phases. We went around the room, and each engineer told the group about his or her experience. The software manager said: "The value was that I learned to define a task and then just give the engineers time to do it without constantly inspecting. . . . It was a training in empowerment." A few of the engineers mentioned that quiet time gave them permission to say "no" and focus on their own work. Specifically, one engineer said:

> I really learned a lot from it. I used to be uncomfortable telling people to go away, and now I feel okay, which enables me to really focus on what I am doing. I used to spend extra time late at night, but now I can get the work done during the day, and spend the extra time on additional work which makes it more worthwhile. . . . The sign gives me the right to tell people to come back, when before I really never felt that was okay. I am still uncomfortable, but I believe that it is now within my rights.

Other engineers spoke about how quiet time forced them to recognize the effects their use of time was having on others. For example, one engineer said: "I always used to worry about my own quiet time. I would reflect on how to get more of it, but this made me think about how I am impacting others. I realize now that it is not just a pursuit for my own quiet time but others' quiet time as well must be considered. It has made me more aware of others' needs and not just my own."

Some engineers noticed a difference in the supervisory style of their managers. Managers no longer constantly checked status or shifted priorities on what looked like a whim. Apparently, managers came to realize that frequent checks on the progress of engineers were unnecessary. As one engineer explained, "I notice a difference in management style. I can be more relaxed now. I do not feel like I am constantly looking over my shoulder. Managers are not constantly standing over me pulling me to do other things."

The division vice-president gave the quiet time study credit for PEARL's on-time product launch. "I do not think we could have made the deadline without this study," he said. "This is a new benchmark."

Despite the positive results for product development, however, and the enhancement of individual productivity, many engineers did not feel that they could use the time savings at home as they had hoped. One engineer expressed the situation well: "I have not been affected in a positive way in terms of my family life. That has not changed at all. Rather I push on the boundary at work until my husband is pissed." For at least one of the managers it was different: "Now I can get my work done in less time. Things I used to have to get done late at night, get done during the normal work day. This allows me more time at home."

Reflecting on Quiet Time

Initially, the software engineers were intrigued by the experiment and willing to suspend their normal ways of working in order to have quiet time, largely because they recognized that continual interruptions made it difficult for them to complete their own work.

For the most part, they were unaware of the reciprocal effect they were having on others. Temporal restructuring taught them that their own work styles can have a negative impact on others; they tend to do to others exactly what they do not like others to do to them. As individuals became more conscientious about their interactions, they interrupted others less and, in turn, found themselves with more uninterrupted time. They had begun to transform the vicious work time cycle into a virtuous one.

With the success of the study came a diminution in the sense of crisis. However, the cultural assumptions about what it takes to succeed at work had not changed. Additional time gained through altering the work patterns was simply poured back into work on individual deliverables. The managers saw no incentive to change the system of rewards. From their perspective, it made economic sense to have individuals work more efficiently for the same period of time and therefore accomplish even more work than before.

Without some sanction for violating quiet time and *without changing the criteria for success,* each engineer has an incentive to interrupt others. The current reward system encourages engineers to do whatever it takes to get their own work done, regardless of the effects on others. Consequently, although collective change in interaction patterns positively affected the group and the group's work process, left on their own, each engineer reverted to his or her old way of working. Both engineers and Ditto suffer as a result.[3]

There are several implications to be drawn from this collaborative attempt to restructure work time collectively. First, it highlights some of the boundary conditions required for effective implementation of quiet time. Phase 1 and Phase 3 indicate that quiet

---

[3] Anthony Giddens (1984) notes that it is possible that the outcome of action is everyone's doing and yet no one's doing. In other words, no one may intentionally cause the outcome, and yet the outcome results from everyone's continued actions. This phenomenon receives the most attention when the unintended consequence results in an undesirable outcome for everyone (Boudon 1982). In such a case, since no one recognizes that the consequence is an outcome of their collective action, all continue to perpetuate the action even though it creates an undesirable outcome for themselves as well as everyone else involved. This is the case of the "tragedy of commons." In post-Roman England, the cattle grazed in a common pasture. Each farmer benefited from maximizing the number of cattle that he owned. Yet, when there were too many cattle, all the grass was eaten and the pasture dried up. The land was destroyed for everyone and all the farmers suffered.

time is possible and desirable. Phase 2 suggests that too much quiet time or too rigid a structure may be counterproductive. Second, the project successfully demonstrates that collective change has the potential to result in a more virtuous—as opposed to vicious—work time cycle, even in a context where there is great time pressure to get products to market. Finally, the results indicate that for long-lasting change, all three components of the vicious work time cycle—individual heroics, constant interruptions, and crisis mentality—must change. The experimental change did not sustain itself because it was not accompanied by cultural change in the criteria for success. Given that the project involved only one small subset of one division of a large corporation, this result is not surprising. After my departure, individuals' behavior was again governed by the corporate reward system, they returned to their old way of working, and most of the short-term gains were lost. The quiet time study suggests that even though everyone may be better off if work patterns are changed, individuals will not alter their work patterns as long as their own deliverables are what matter most. In the end, for most individuals, the desire to succeed will overwhelm their willingness to cooperate.[4]

---

[4] This finding is supported by the early work of Alexander Mintz (1951). Mintz used laboratory experiments to confirm the theory that the reward structure and not emotional excitement is chiefly responsible for nonadaptive behavior of groups. In these experiments subjects had to take cones out of a bottle. Only one cone could be taken out at a time and the neck of the bottle was easily blocked by attempting to remove too many cones simultaneously; the cones came out only if the subjects cooperated with one another. In the majority of cases, serious "traffic jams" resulted when individual rewards and fines were attached. Emotional facilitation had little, if any, effect on the results. Mintz concluded that as soon as individuals are rewarded, even to a small degree, for their own personal achievement they act in a way that may be detrimental to the group and ultimately to themselves.

11

New Work Practices: Benefits for Corporations, Individuals, and Families

This book set out to explore the necessity of the long hours that postindustrial work settings require. The deleterious consequences of long hours of work for individuals, families, and communities have previously been documented. What has not been challenged is the assumption that long hours are necessary to get the work done, especially in a world where speed is becoming increasingly critical to corporate success. There has been some recognition that stress and burnout may be disadvantageous to the corporation because employees may become less committed, decide to leave, or get fired. This kind of turnover may hurt the corporation in the longer term. What I have documented in this book, however, are the additional, and quite significant shorter-term costs to the corporation of the current way of using time at work. The lack of helping, the constant interruptions, and the perpetual crises clearly make it harder to develop a product. Whether these costs exceed the benefits that result from all the pressure was investigated in Part III. The quiet time study indicates that productivity could be enhanced by structuring work time to permit engineers some intervals to work alone without interruptions. This finding implies that the costs of the current way of using time indeed exceed the benefits. The chapters in Part III further show that change must be collective and must address all the elements of the vicious cycle. Ultimately, the criteria for success will have to change.

The promising implication is that collective change could benefit corporations, individuals, and families. The work process could be made more efficient and effective. At the same time, individuals could succeed at work and still have time left for responsibilities outside of work; people might not have to choose so definitively between their work and their home life. To make the necessary changes, however, will require a shift from a system that rewards individual heroics and long hours to a system that rewards individuals' contributions to their teams without the accompanying emphasis on visible work hours. That is, there must be a shift in emphasis from individual to collective achievement and there must be a sharing of the resulting gains in efficiency between individuals and the corporation.

Step 1: A Shift toward Collective Achievement

To suggest a need for a shift in emphasis from the individual to the collective is not new. The pendulum has swung from a focus at work on individual goals to a focus on collective goals. Many publications and presentations in the 1990s have touted the importance of teamwork and team rewards. Indeed, there has been much emphasis on facilitating interdependencies by breaking down functional barriers in organizations, co-locating individuals, and encouraging employee communication and accessibility at work. To date, however, the importance of the *timing* of these interactions has been overlooked. What is distinct about my findings is the recognition not only that interdependencies themselves are crucial to the work process but also that it matters when and how people interact.

To promote interactions that foster achievement of the group's output rather than individual's output, there needs to be recognition of individuals' contributions to the larger goals of the project and not just their ability to complete their own individual deliverables on time. This kind of recognition will require cultural change, change in the underlying assumptions about what it takes to succeed. It will also require change in the process through which individuals decide how they use their time at work. Instead of individuals making unilateral decisions about how to use time, employees will need to work collectively to determine how each person's time use can best benefit the group. There must be change in the way people think about working together as well as change in the reward system. Both are necessary to create a shift from individual to collective achievement.

This shift should give rise to a new generation of time management. In his best-selling book, *The Seven Habits of Highly Effective People,* Stephen Covey gives a cogent history of four generations of time management. The first generation recognized that individuals have a problem dealing with multiple demands on their time and energy and, introduced the idea of keeping notes and checklists as reminders. The second generation recognized the need for planning and introduced calendars and appointment books to help individuals plan and keep track of future commitments. The third generation identified the importance of efficiently and effectively delegating, planning, prioritizing, and saying "no." Fourth-generation time management showed the need not only to prioritize what is on one's to-do list but also to consider whether the "correct" activities are on the list; the idea is that people should prioritize activities not according to urgency but according to importance, given one's principles, personal missions, roles, and goals.

Proponents of all four generations of time management assert that individuals can make the necessary changes in their lives to gain control of the situation if they will only invest the effort to master time-management tactics (e.g., Brooks and Mullins 1989; Jones 1993; and Griessman 1994). For example, according to Alec Mackenzie (1990), "The biggest single time waster, worldwide, is telephone interruptions. The person who has not thought about this will say, 'But that's not *my* fault; these people are calling *me.*' Yes, but you permit the interruption; you take the call" (p. 7). The promise is that if *you* make the necessary changes in *your* life then *you* will personally benefit from greater success at work and greater control over *your* life.

The fundamental problem with the first four generations of time management is that they promote individual-level changes. At best, these techniques address the fallout of the vicious work time cycle, not the cycle itself. For example, to decrease interruptions by creating periods of quiet time for oneself (a third-generation technique) may help engineers cope but does not alter engineers' incentives to interrupt others, and therefore does not mitigate the crisis mentality or the demand for individual heroics. Furthermore, however desirable, it is often impossible for individual engineers to reduce the number of urgent but not important demands by planning better and including extra time for contingencies (a fourth-generation technique). Engineers simply cannot conclude that their manager has unnecessarily created a crisis and therefore decide not to respond to it. Rather, engineers caught in the vicious work time cycle are rewarded for conquering the crises thrown at them, and those engineers who do not respond risk being punished by the organizational reward system. Reducing the number of urgent items one faces would require altering both engineers' interaction patterns and the system that rewards individual heroics. In other words, the vicious work time cycle itself must be addressed.

I do not mean to assert that my conclusions in this book necessarily indicate engineers should not use the techniques promoted by fourth-generation time management. There is nothing wrong with trying to prioritize activities based on importance rather than urgency. But if individual efficiency increases at the expense of collective efficiency, then even bigger temporal problems are created.

A fifth generation of time management focused on the collective should address the inefficiencies of interacting. Among the engineers I studied, each had his or her own individual deliverables, but they also depended on one another to put the product together. They could not complete their work without interacting. It is the inefficiency of these necessary but unstructured interactions which must be managed.

Unstructured interdependencies and the vicious cycle to which they contribute likely exist in many types of work. In particular, I am thinking of occupations such as consulting, investment banking, and corporate law, where individuals are part of a collective that depends on both independent cognitive work and interdependent action to succeed. If in these settings, despite the need for collective activity, rewards are based on individual achievements and/or work practices are thought about at the individual level, then these groups should benefit as well from fifth-generation time management.

In contrast, I would not expect the same inefficiencies (or benefits from change) to exist for self-employed individuals who can isolate themselves, turn on their answering machines, and focus fully on their "real work." For example, psychotherapists can ensure that they are undisturbed while seeing patients. Similarly, I would not expect these findings to apply to any type of work in which individuals are given an independent task and told how to execute it. When tasks are well defined and actions independent, interaction is not crucial. In these cases, there would be no reason to expect loss of efficiency due to interactions. A prime example would be assembly-line employees whose work is completely structured by mechanical rules. It is in a situation that requires individuals to work together in unspecified ways that the possibility of inefficient interdependencies arises.

In documenting and prescribing change for these inefficiencies in the work process, I have outlined what scientific management for the postindustrial firm might look like. In essence, this study of time use shows ways to make certain types of workers more efficient. The findings should be useful to those who manage employees whose work involves both an individual cognitive component and an unstructured interdependent component.

Step 2: Sharing the Gains

My motivation in conducting this research *was not* to look for ways to make knowledge workers more efficient but to understand how they use their time at work and whether they need to work such long hours. My findings indicate that inefficiencies at work contribute to extra, unnecessary hours of work. The implication is that at least in certain work settings, if the way time is used were altered, more work could get done in less time, leaving more time for other things.

A key issue, however, is what will happen with the time saved from any gains in efficiency. This question brings us to the second step of the changes I advocate. If managers alter the system that rewards individual heroics and interaction patterns change, but managers do not simultaneously reduce their demand for long hours of work, then managers will gain *all* the benefits of increased efficiency. In other words, just taking the first step will merely facilitate people working more efficiently for the same long hours.

However, on a practical level, it is not clear that the corporation could reap all the benefits. Sharing the gains in efficiency is probably critical if the change is to succeed. It is not at all apparent how efficient employees can be made. It may be that interruptions provide employees the necessary respite to enable them to sustain their long work hours. Increasing efficiency, by improving interaction patterns, will provide employees more time to concentrate on their individual cognitive work, but deep concentration may not be sustainable through the long hours currently worked. Certainly at some point, one would expect employees to reach their maximum productivity, beyond which more time at work would not continue to increase their output and might even decrease it. It therefore may be that the outcome that yields the highest productivity indeed requires a shorter work day.

It is important to keep in mind as well that the quiet time study itself was a collaborative project that intertwined managers' interest in getting the product to market as soon as possible with engineers' interest in enhancing balance in their lives between work and life outside of work. It may well be that the engineers were willing to participate because of their own interest in having more uninterrupted time at work. It might be that satisfying their interests was critical, and had it not been an initial objective of the study, the change would not have succeeded. Certainly what I heard when I went back to Ditto six months after PEARL launched supported this supposition. The engineers told me that their next product had recently slipped behind schedule. In an attempt to speed up the process, their managers had again tried to implement quiet time. One engineer expressed a sentiment I heard from many: "Quiet time alone doesn't work. The managers were not taking our interests into account. They were not trying to make life better for us. They were just trying to get whatever productivity enhancements they could. They don't get it. They don't get what you were doing here. . . . We had no incentive to abide by quiet time. . . . No one did."

Managers' failure to reap the productivity gains without taking the engineers' interests into account has profound implications for understanding what is needed to make an effective change in work culture. The success of the project apparently derived at least in part from the engineers' sense that their interests were being taken into account. It therefore may be that for anyone—the corporation, its employees or their families—to benefit from better use of time at work, the gains from increasing efficiency will have to be shared.

Benefits to the Corporation

Even if both steps are necessary and the gains in efficiency do have to be shared, the corporation stands to benefit from shifting the criteria for success away from the individual and toward the collective. Most obviously, if people could get the same amount of work done in less time, they would have more time to spend on their family lives and themselves. As a result, they would likely lead healthier, less stressful lives. In the short term individuals with primary responsibility at home, mostly women, would be more likely to be retained by the corporation. In the longer term, individuals, in general, would be less prone to burnout. Although managers often ignore the negative effects of burnout and the implications of losing people who prefer more balanced lives, there are high costs for the bottom line associated with the loss of some of the best people after only a few years. Moreover, the corporation stands to benefit from change in another crucial way. Making time use more efficient will reduce both crises and interruptions. Better planning will be possible, leading to higher-quality output.

At Ditto, attempts to promote more time for life outside of work are perceived as antithetical to corporate productivity. My research indicates, on the contrary, that the two goals can be mutually supportive. If managers do take both the steps I am recommending, the results should be an organization where more employees can take advantage of flexible options without hindering their careers. At the same time, changes in work behavior should enhance the quality of the work and the longer-term potential of the work force.

AFTERWORD

Two Years Later

Two years have gone by. I no longer have access to Building 113. I must wait at the entrance for someone to come and escort me through the main door. As I wait, I wonder, Will the people I know still be there? What will I do all day? Who will take time out of their busy schedule to talk to me?

Once inside, I am relieved. I see many familiar faces, and everyone stops to say hello. They ask why I am back and tell me that not much has changed. The pressure to produce is as great as ever. The engineers explain that PEARL has not done well in the marketplace. One manager admits, "Color laser printing did not take the market by storm as we had hoped it would." As a result, the engineers still work in a division that is losing money and is under immense pressure to produce a profit.

Twelve of the original seventeen members of the PEARL software group remain in the division. Eleven of the twelve are now working on a new color laser printer that is supposed to have much better image quality and is targeted to sell at less than half the cost of PEARL. The hope is that with a low enough price and more effective marketing the product will sell better.

The engineers say that the biggest difference in their new product's development is their own attitude. As one of the engineers put it:

It is the same old same old. The only difference is that we are numb to it now. It has all been going on for such a long time. . . . The attitude is yah, yah, yah. I know there is another deadline. Leave me alone. I am doing the best I can. . . . We are all doing the best we can, but sometimes it just isn't good enough. . . . I used to put in more time. Now, it isn't that I am not working hard, I am not slacking off, but I just don't care as much. Before I was more interested in the work. I feel like the work is getting old. I am tired of it. I just won't do it now. . . . I have more going on in my life outside of work.

The division vice-president has a very different perspective. He thinks that there have been significant positive changes. He acknowledges that the product team was "driven into the ground working on PEARL." He blames the product manager who is no longer with the division. The division vice-president says he personally is trying to make things better: "I am trying to revitalize my staff." With the most recent product, he says he intentionally slipped the schedule in order to avoid pushing his people beyond their limits again. He adds that he should have slipped the schedule on PEARL, as well. "It wasn't worth what we did to our people."

While, the engineers recognize the schedule slip, they explain it in a very different way. They say that the product was so far behind schedule that the management team had no choice but to slip the schedule. The team simply could not have made the original date. As one engineer put it, "There is no slack in the schedule. There is no way we could have made it, no matter how hard we tried. It simply would not have been possible." From the engineers' perspective, the schedule is still too ambitious, and there is still too much work and too much stress.

Among the PEARL software engineers who work on this new product, Matt and Sarah have both been promoted to project team leaders, and both now manage four engineers. Sarah finds the work more demanding than ever. She and her husband have agreed to cut out all activities other than work so that they can spend more time at home together. Sarah says she wants to be part of her daughter's childhood and she wants a second child. For now, she adds, "I'm exhausted. I just want some time to sleep." For

Matt, the biggest problem is learning how to delegate. He explains, "I ask my team to do things, but if they don't want to, I always end up doing the tasks myself." As a result, he says he still works very long hours.

Jane is now a systems engineer in the division, which means that no one reports to her directly as engineers do to Matt and Sarah. She does, however, have more technical responsibility than she did. She is also eight and a half months' pregnant with her second child. Jane continues to accept the tradeoffs she is forced to make. She says, "I have accepted I will never be a star here. . . . That is OK with me."

Laura has received another promotion. She now manages fifty people and reports directly to the division vice-president. She also now comes in four mornings a week at 2 A.M. or "as many mornings as my husband will let me." Laura says, "I love my new job. I work fifteen-hour days, but I rarely work over the weekend . . . except to check my messages. I have learned to dread Monday mornings if I haven't checked messages and responded to any urgent calls from my boss."

As for the other members of the PEARL team, five have left the division. Milton, the product manager, and Allan, one of the three project team leaders, have moved on to new divisions within Ditto. The other three team members have left the company altogether. Max is gone. He moved to a new job with more responsibility and more opportunity. Kate is gone too. Soon after transferring to the new division, she filed for divorce, and later she moved closer to her parents. Chris has also left for a better job closer to home.

None of those who have left has made much effort to keep in touch. A couple of e-mail notes have been received, but that is about it. For those who remain, life is much the same. The division still faces great pressure to succeed; deadlines remain extremely tight; and managers continue to demand long hours. Crises and individual heroics proliferate, and so the vicious work time cycle keeps on spinning.

METHODOLOGICAL APPENDIX

A Research Tale

The bulk of the research for this book was conducted between 1991 and 1995 while I was at the Sloan School of Management at the Massachusetts Institute of Technology. I was part of a research team sponsored by the Ford Foundation to study gender equity and work/life issues in postindustrial American corporations.[1] Access to Ditto was based on an agreement between Ditto and the Ford Foundation. The research team chose Ditto because of its reputation as a leader in implementing flexible work policies to address employees' work/life conflicts.

Because our official approval to conduct research at Ditto came from the most senior managers, both the managers and the engineers apparently felt obligated to facilitate our research. The mere fact that the CEO had sanctioned the research seems to have fostered a willingness to participate that I do not think we would have received otherwise. We repeatedly emphasized to those with whom we came into contact that we were not funded by the corporation or aligned with the management in any way.

The other factor that played a critical role in gaining the engineers' support was that we came from MIT. There is no

---

[1] The research team included six other members besides myself: Lotte Bailyn, Deborah Kolb, Susan Eaton, Joyce Fletcher, Maureen Harvey, and Robin Johnson.

institution that the engineers we studied hold in higher regard. We benefited from their respect for MIT, and the engineers' supportive, relatively open, attitude that resulted provided unique opportunities for both data collection and experimentation within the company.

Data on Life at Ditto

In the fall of 1991 I started visiting Ditto. For the next two years, I and several members of my research team, made visits once every month or two. I kept abreast of affairs in the division, and I became acquainted with members of the division's senior management team, some of its more junior managers, and many of the division's mechanical engineers. I came to understand much about the work, and the work/life conflicts of members of the division. During my first two years at Ditto, I never met any of the seventeen software engineers I later studied.

In September 1993 I began a nine-month stay as a participant observer of the software group. I "moved" to Ditto as PEARL was being funded (September 1993) and stayed through its launch (June 1994), spending an average of four days a week on site. My typical routine was to arrive at Ditto between seven and nine o'clock, depending on what activities I had planned for that day. I usually remained there until at least six o'clock and often until eight or nine in the evening. Although I did not typically engage in planned research activities after five or six o'clock, I found that typing my field notes at Ditto, rather than in my hotel room, facilitated casual but revealing conversations with the engineers and the managers about the trials and tribulations they had encountered during the day. Moreover, late-night presence gave me a more accurate sense of the actual hours individuals worked at different stages of product development.[2] It also seemed to bring me more respect because the engineers perceived that I too was working hard.

---

[2] It is hard not to notice my own long hours of work. I struggle to make it a world where I too do not feel compelled to put in so much time.

I spent much of each day wandering around, talking to people and observing their daily activities. I had an office in the same corridor, where I would type my field notes on a laptop computer. Even when typing notes, I left my office door open. I sat facing the door, looking up when people walked by, inviting conversation if an engineer or manager chose to enter.

In addition to being present and available to talk to the engineers, I conducted interviews and attended meetings. Initially, I engaged each of the seventeen members of the software team in one- to two-hour interviews, in which I gathered background information about members of the group and gained a preliminary understanding of individuals' perceptions about work and work/life issues. Later, I shadowed engineers—some for part of a day, some for a whole workday, and others for several workdays—to get a sense of how they accomplished their work. Moreover, I sat for hours in each of the software labs observing and talking to the engineers at work and listening to the "natural" interactions that occurred in the labs.

I also used a tracking device to document the work of the engineers more extensively than my notes allowed. On randomly selected days, I asked each member of the software group to wear a digital watch that beeped on the hour. At each beep, I asked the engineer to write down everything he or she had done in the previous hour. I encouraged the engineers to write interactions down as they occurred and to use the beeps as an extra reminder to do so. Engineers were given the watch the night before and asked to track their activities from the time they woke up until they went to bed. This technique provided information not only on their patterns of interaction at work but also on their lives and responsibilities outside of work.

I asked each engineer to track his or her activities on three different, randomly selected days. Three or four engineers were asked to track on any given day. I would follow the tracking with a debriefing interview the next day, which I taped and transcribed. I began each interview by asking the engineer to elaborate on the activities listed on his or her log sheet. For each interactive activity, I asked the engineers to identify with whom they had interacted, who initiated the interaction, what the purpose was, whether it was helpful or disruptive to them, whether they perceived it as helpful or disruptive to the other(s) involved, and finally, whether the interaction could have been postponed or avoided. The debriefings also provided a wealth of information not only about the actual day-to-day sequence of the work but also about key events at work and in the engineers' lives outside of work.

Data on Performance

At the end of each year, Ditto senior managers decide on employee raises for the year. Categories are set, and designated percentages of employees are placed into each category. Division managers rank their top and bottom software engineers to help determine raises. This list is available only to managers involved in the process. At my request, I was given a copy of this list. Each of the engineers also gave me permission to copy his/her performance evaluation. I further had access to the data on the pay raises each engineer received. Kate, the engineer whose case is described in Chapter 9, gave me permission to look through her complete personnel file.

Data on Life outside of Ditto

As part of my research, I wanted to understand the engineers' lives outside of work. I asked the married engineers to let me visit their homes and interview their spouses. Most of the engineers agreed, some with apparent enthusiasm. Of the twelve software engineers I studied, seven were married and I interviewed five of the seven spouses. Furthermore, the spouses of all three project team leaders, the independent contributor, the software manager, the product manager, and the division vice-president welcomed me into their homes.

I made twelve home visits. Each lasted anywhere from two to six hours. In the case of the male engineers, I visited all but one of their homes in the afternoon and interviewed their wives before the engineers came home. In two of these cases, I joined the families for dinner after the interview. In the case of the four female engineers, all of their husbands worked full-time. I therefore went home with the women after work, took part in picking up the children from day care, preparing meals, and putting the children to bed. Though the engineers were home in all these cases, I conducted the interviews in a separate room for privacy. During home visits, when both spouses were present, I also conducted three-way discussions about the issues of work-family balance.

Data from Social Events

I participated in many social events. I went to lunch with the engineers on a regular basis. Although several of the engineers (and all the project team leaders) did not take time off for lunch, those who did tended to do one of three things: eat in the main cafeteria in a Ditto building a ten-minute walk away; go to the lab and play chess with several other engineers; or spend the time alone running errands or going to the library. I tended to join the first group of engineers. Occasionally, I watched the second group play chess. The game was intense as played at Ditto. The matches were timed, and the players were not allowed to speak. Although it was fascinating that the same four engineers chose to spend their lunchtime in this way day after day, there was not much more to be learned about their work from observing them. I found lunch conversations in the main cafeteria more informative. The engineers spoke about their own lives and about the "events" occurring at Ditto. It is noteworthy that none of the women in the group regularly went to lunch. When I went to lunch in the main cafeteria it was almost always with three to ten male engineers.

In addition to these standard lunches, about once a month an engineer would decide they should all "go out for lunch." The engineer would gather a group together, and the group would head off (usually) to a local Chinese restaurant about a twenty-minute drive from Ditto. A big group of engineers, including some of the "chess crowd" and some of the women who did not typically take time for lunch would attend. I too would go along.

In addition to lunchtimes, I joined the engineers on several occasions for "happy hour" on Friday nights at one of the bars downtown. I also attended the official celebrations at the end of the project including a launch party and a three-day bus trip to New York City, where PEARL was unveiled at PC Exposition. Opportunities such as "happy hours" and the New York trip gave me a chance to talk more freely with the engineers and get a sense of who they are and how they interact with each other socially.

Reflecting on My Stay

I very much enjoyed my research role at Ditto. It was my job to listen, and so, regardless of what I was doing or how I was feeling, I made myself available when the engineers wanted to tell me something. I found myself privy to many unsolicited conversations whether engineers had something specific they felt I should know or they were simply looking for a break in their work and wanted someone to chat with. By being an active listener, I developed relationships with individuals at many levels of the organization. I found that I often would hear the same story from several vantage points. It was not uncommon for an engineer, a project team leader, and a manager to give me their personal viewpoints about a single incident.

Writing up My Findings

When I arrived home from my field stay in July 1994, I found myself with thousands of pages of field notes, hundreds of transcribed interviews and daily logs, survey data, and my personal experiences to interpret. My next step was not traditional. I did not start mining my data for themes. Rather, inspired by Arlie Hochschild's book *The Second Shift*, I started writing stories. I wrote seventeen stories, one about each individual I had studied. I wrote about their work styles, their family lives, and whatever character traits stood out. Once I completed this exercise, I looked for similarities and differences among the people I had described. I chose these characteristics as themes I wanted to home in on in the data analysis.

Only at this point did I follow the more traditional guidelines suggested by Glaser and Strauss (1967) and Miles and Huberman (1984). I developed empirically grounded sets of categories and followed an iterative process fitting observations to categories. As new observations arose, I continually made choices whether to retain, revise, or discard particular categories (or category sets).

After considerable analysis of the themes that emerged from the stories as well as other themes specifically about work patterns and perceptions about what it takes to succeed, I returned to the stories I had written and chose the portions I would actually keep intact in the text. In the end, I have given five individuals more chance to speak than I gave the others. I chose these individuals because I felt they exemplified the themes I wanted to highlight, but all the stories are woven into the themes of the book.

REFERENCES

Baddeley, A. D. 1972. Selective attention and performance in dangerous environments. *British Journal of Psychology* 63:537–46.

Bailyn, L. 1993. *Breaking the mold: Women, men, and time in the new corporate world.* New York: Free Press.

Bailyn, L., et al. 1996. Re-linking work and family: A catalyst for organizational change. Sloan Working Paper 3892–96.

Barthol, R. P., and N. D. Ku. 1959. Regression under stress to first learned behavior. *Journal of Abnormal and Social Psychology* 59:134–36.

Bell, D. 1973. *The coming of post industrial society: A venture into social forecasting.* New York: Basic Books.

Bellah, R. N., et al. 1985. *Habits of the heart: Individualism and commitment in American life.* Berkeley: University of California Press.

Boudon, R. 1982. *The unintended consequences of social action.* New York: St. Martin's Press.

Braverman, H. 1974. *Labor and monopoly capital: The degradation of work in the twentieth century.* New York: Monthly Review Press.

Brooks, F. P. 1982. *The mythical man-month.* Reading, Mass.: Addison-Wesley.

Brooks, W. T., and T. W. Mullins. 1989. *High impact time management.* Englewood Cliffs, N.J.: Prentice-Hall.

Bucciarelli, L. L. 1988. Engineering design process. In *Making time: Ethnographies of high-technology organizations,* 92–122, edited by F. A. Dubinskas. Philadelphia: Temple University Press.

Burawoy, M. 1979. *Manufacturing consent.* Chicago: University of Chicago Press.

Covey, S. 1989. *The seven habits of highly effective people.* New York: Simon and Schuster.

Crawford, S. 1989. *Technical workers in an advanced society.* Cambridge: Cambridge University Press.

Dertouzos, M. L., et al. 1989. *Made in America: Regaining the productive edge.* Boston: MIT Press.

Easterbrook, J. A. 1959. The effect of emotion on cue utilization and the organization of behavior. *Psychological Review* 66:183–201.

Edwards, R. C. 1979. *Contested terrain.* New York: Basic Books.

Evans, P., and F. Bartolome. 1980. *Must success cost so much? The human toll of corporate life.* New York: Basic Books.

Fassel, D. 1990. *Working ourselves to death: The high cost of workaholism and the rewards of recovery.* New York: Harper Collins.

Fletcher, J. 1994. Toward a theory of relational practice in organizations: A feminist reconstruction of "real" work. Ph.D. diss., Boston University.

Giddens, A. 1984. *The constitution of society.* Berkeley: University of California Press.

Glaser, B. G., and A. L. Strauss. 1967. *The discovery of grounded theory: Strategies for qualitative research*. New York: Aldine.

Goffman, E. 1967. *Interaction ritual*. Chicago: Aldine.

———. 1983. The interaction order. *American Sociological Review* 48:1–17.

Griessman, B. E. 1994. *Time tactics of very successful people*. New York: McGraw-Hill.

Hayghe, H. V., and S. W. Cromartie. 1991. Working woman: A chart book. U.S. Department of Labor, Bureau of Labor Statistics, *Bulletin* 2385 (August).

Hochschild, A. R. 1989. *The second shift: Working parents and the revolution at home*. New York: Avon Books.

———. 1997. *The time bind: When work becomes home and home becomes work*. New York: Metropolitan Books.

Jackall, R. 1988. *Moral mazes: The world of corporate managers*. New York: Oxford University Press.

Jones, J. W. 1993. *High speed management: Time based strategies for managers and organizations*. San Francisco: Jossey-Bass.

Kidder, T. 1981. *The soul of a new machine*. New York: Avon Books.

Kraft, P. 1979. The industrialization of computer programming: From programming to "software production." In *Case studies in the labor process*, edited by A. Zimbalist. New York: Monthly Review Press.

Kunda, G. 1992. *Engineering culture*. Philadelphia: Temple University Press.

Landers, R. M., J. Rebitzer, and L. J. Taylor. 1996. Rat race redux: Adverse selection in the determination of work hours in law firms. *American Economic Review* 86: 329–348.

Lawler, E. E., III. 1986. *High involvement management: Participative strategies for improving organizational performance*. San Francisco: Jossey-Bass.

Leidner, R. 1988. Home work: A study in the interaction of work and family organization. *Research in Sociology of Work* 4:69–94.

Levering, R., and M. Moskowitz. 1993. *The 100 best companies to work for in America*. Reading, Mass.: Addison-Wesley.

Lewin, K. 1948. *Resolving social conflicts*. New York: Harper and Row.

Mackenzie, A. 1990. *The time trap*. New York: Amacom.

Mandler, G. 1982. Stress and thought processes. In *Handbook of stress*, 84–104, edited by L. Goldberger and S. Breznitz. New York: Free Press.

McIlwee, J. S., and J. G. Robinson. 1992. *Women in engineering: Gender, power, and workplace culture*. Albany: State University of New York Press.

Miles, M. B., and A. M. Huberman. 1984. *Qualitative data analysis: A source book of new methods*. Beverly Hills, Calif.: Sage.

Mintz, A. 1951. Nonadaptive group behavior. *Journal of Abnormal and Social Psychology* 46:150–59.

Mintzberg, H. 1973. *The nature of managerial work*. New York: Harper and Row.

Moore-Ede, M. 1993. *The twenty-four-hour society*. Reading, Mass.: Addison-Wesley.

Perin, C. 1991. The moral fabric of the office: Panopticon discourse and schedule flexibilities. *Research in Sociology of Organizations* 8:241–68.

Perlow, L. 1994. The myth of "real engineering": An exploration of what it really takes to get the job done. Sloan Working Paper 3373.

———. 1995a. Putting the work back into work-family. *Group and Organization Management* 20:227–39.

———. 1995b. The time famine: The unintended consequence of the way time is used at work. Ph.D. diss., MIT.

——. Forthcoming. Boundary control: The social ordering of work and family life in a high-tech corporation. *Administrative Science Quarterly.*

——. 1996. The time famine: Towards a sociology of work time. *Academy of Management Best Paper Proceedings.*

——, and L. Bailyn. 1997. The senseless submergence of difference: Engineers, their work, and their careers. In *Between craft and science: Technical work in the United States,* edited by S. Barley and J. Orr. Ithaca, N.Y.: IRL Press.

Roy, D. 1960. Banana time. *Human Organization* 18:158–68.

Sacks, H. E., A. Schegloff, and G. Jefferson. 1974. A simplest systematics for the organization of turn-taking for conversation. *Language* 50 (4):696–735.

Savage, C. M. 1990. *Fifth generation management.* Digital Press.

Schegloff, E. 1992. On talk and its institutional occasions. In *Talk at work,* edited by P. Drew and J. Heritage. New York: Cambridge University Press.

Schein, E. 1987. *The clinical perspective in fieldwork.* Newbury Park, Calif.: Sage.

Schor, J. B. 1992. *The overworked American: The unexpected decline of leisure.* Basic Books.

Shamir, B., and I. Salomon. 1985. Work-at-home and the quality of working life. *Academy of Management Review* 10 (3): 455–64.

Silvestri, G., and J. Lukasiewicz. 1991. Occupational employment projections. *Monthly Labor Review* (November): 64–94.

Stalk, G., and T. M. Hout. 1990. *Competing against time: How time based competition is reshaping global markets.* New York: Free Press.

Swiss, D. J., and J. P. Walker. 1993. *Women and the work-family dilemma: How today's professional women are finding solutions.* New York: John Wiley and Sons.

Tocqueville, A. de 1969. *Democracy in America.* Translated by G. Lawrence. Edited by J. P. Mayer. New York: Doubleday, Anchor Books.

Tucker, J. T. 1991. *Managing the future: Ten driving forces of change for the '90s.* New York: Putnam.

Van Maanen, J. 1988. *Tales of the field: On writing ethnography.* Chicago: University of Chicago Press.

——. 1990. On asking for help. Unpublished notes.

——, and S. Barley. 1984. Occupational communities: Culture and control in organizations. In *Research in Organizational Behavior* 6:287–365, edited by L. L. Cummings and B. M. Staw. Greenwich, Conn.: JAI Press.

Watchel, P. 1967. Conceptions of broad and narrow attention. *Psychological Bulletin* 68:417–29.

Weltman, G., J. Smith, and G. Egstrom. 1971. Perceptual narrowing during simulated pressure-chamber exposure. *Human Factors* 13:99–107.

Wheelwright, S. C., and K. B. Clark. 1992. *Revolutionizing product development.* New York: Free Press.

Whyte, W. H., Jr. 1956. *The organization man.* New York: Simon and Schuster.

Zachary, G. P. 1994. *ShowStopper: The breakneck race to create Windows NT and the next generation at Microsoft.* New York: Free Press.

Zajonc, R. 1965. Social facilitation. *Science* 149:269–74.

Zerubaval, E. 1979. *Patterns of time in hospital life.* Chicago: University of Chicago Press.

Zuboff, S. 1988. *In the age of the smart machine.* New York: Basic Books.

Zussman, R. 1985. *Mechanics of the middle class.* Berkeley: University of California Press.

INDEX